Polikarpov Biplane Fighters

Yefim Gordon and Keith Dexter

Midland Publishing

Polikarpov's Biplane Fighters
© 2002 Yefim Gordon and Keith Dexter
ISBN 1 85780 141 5

Published by Midland Publishing
4 Watling Drive, Hinckley, LE10 3EY, England
Tel: 01455 254 490   Fax: 01455 254 495
E-mail: midlandbooks@compuserve.com

Midland Publishing is an imprint of
Ian Allan Publishing Ltd

Worldwide distribution (except North America):
Midland Counties Publications
4 Watling Drive, Hinckley, LE10 3EY, England
Telephone: 01455 254 450   Fax: 01455 233 737
E-mail: midlandbooks@compuserve.com
www.midlandcountiessuperstore.com

North American trade distribution:
Specialty Press Publishers & Wholesalers Inc.
39966 Grand Avenue, North Branch, MN 55056, USA
Tel: 651 277 1400   Fax: 651 277 1203
Toll free telephone: 800 895 4585
www.specialtypress.com

© 2002 Midland Publishing
Design concept and layout
by Polygon Press Ltd (Moscow, Russia)
Colour artwork © Vladimir Titov & Sergey Yershov

This book is illustrated with photos from the
archives of Yefim Gordon, Mikhail Maslov and
the Russian Aviation Research Trust

Printed in England by
Ian Allan Printing Ltd
Riverdene Business Park, Molesey Road,
Hersham, Surrey, KT12 4RG

Title page photograph:
**With the landing gear retracted, the I-153
was quite an elegant aeroplane.**

Contents

**Below: Red Army Air Force I-153s taxy out for a
ground attack sortie. They are armed with eight
(or six, in the case of the aircraft on the right) 82-mm
RS-82 unguided rockets. The foremost aircraft is
unusual in having the engine cooling shutters
removed, exposing the crankcase and cylinders.**

Introduction

Although known in the Soviet Union in the mid-1930s as 'the King of Fighters', Nikolai Nikolayevich Polikarpov's rise to this eminence had not been an easy one. After graduation from the St. Petersburg Polytechnic Institute in 1916 he was employed at the Russo-Baltic Carriage Works (RBVZ – *Roossko-baltiyskiy vagonnyy zavod*) where he worked under Igor' I. Sikorski. Five months after the 1917 October Revolution he joined the Military Air Fleet Board and by September 1918 had become the manager of the technical department at the Duks aircraft factory. The enterprise was located on the edge of an airfield in a place now known as Khodynka, then situated in the north-western suburbs of Moscow. This airfield is now located nearly in the centre of the city; on its perimeter lie the OKBs of Sukhoi and Il'yushin, as well as the former Duks factory which has been repeatedly expanded and rebuilt to become the famous *zavod* No. 30 '*Znamya Truda*' (Banner of Labour) and now known as MAPO.

Drawings of the British de Havilland D.H.4 had been supplied to Russia in 1917, before the revolution, and Polikarpov's first major project was to redesign this aircraft for manufacture with locally made materials, engines and components. However, before this project had been completed the authorities, who were by then more impressed by the examples of the D.H.9a that had been acquired, ordered him to modify the D.H.4 drawings so that an aircraft more akin to the D.H.9a could be produced. Furthermore it was to be capable of carrying out a wider range of tasks. The resultant aircraft was powered by a copy of the 400-hp (298-kW) Liberty engine and, whilst outwardly resembling the D.H.9a, was in fact a completely new design. Known to the Soviet Air Force as the R-1 (R = [*samolyot-*] *razvedchik*, reconnaissance aircraft), it was serially produced in large quantities, with approximately 2,800 being manufactured before production ceased in 1931. This task had a profound effect on Polikarpov who, for the rest of his life, strove to design aeroplanes utilising locally produced materials of which wood was the most readily available; duralumin did not enter the equation, as it was in short supply until the end of World War Two.

The civil war and intervention of foreign armies rendered the recovery of the Soviet aircraft industry slow and painful but in January 1923 an aircraft design office was created at the former 'Duks' factory, about to be redesignated GAZ-1 (*gosoodarstvennyy aviatsionnyy zavod*, state aircraft factory) and Polikarpov was appointed its manager. He lost no time and set about designing a biplane fighter powered by a Liberty engine but, frustratingly, on 6th February 1923 he was transferred to the design office of Glavkoavia (an acronym for the 'Main Management of the Amalgamated Aircraft Factories') and his place at GAZ-1 was taken by Dmitriy P. Grigorovich. The proposed fighter was never built owing to a complete lack of enthusiasm on the part of the GAZ-1 management.

The 1920s evolved into a decade of great transition for the aircraft industry. It was during this period, in August 1924, that Polikarpov was transferred back to GAZ-1. In his new role he encompassed the jobs of production manager and head of the factory design office where he replaced Grigorovich. Polikarpov significantly improved the efficiency of the design office by dividing it into several sections, each performing a separate task for which its manager was accountable.

Influenced by the layout of a captured Junkers monoplane, Polikarpov's first fighter to reach the hardware stage was the IL-400 (*istrebitel'* [*s dvigatelem*] Liberty [*moschnost'yu*] 400 [*loshadinykh sil*], fighter with a 400-hp Liberty engine) which was completed by August 1923. This time Polikarpov had diplomatically taken the precaution of inviting I. M. Kostkin, the production manager of GAZ-1, to be joint leader of the project team.

At the national level reorganisations were also taking place and trusts had become the favoured organisation for controlling factories within industries. This led to the replacement of Glavkoavia by Aviatrest on 7th January 1925 and the creation of a combined design office and experimental department, the OSS (*Otdel sookhoputnykh samolyotov* – Landplane Department) headed by Polikarpov. After the establishment of the Central Design Bureau of Aviatrust (TsKB Aviatresta) on 19th September 1926 it became its landplane component and was later renamed OPO-1 (*opytnyy otdel*, experimental department).

Polikarpov, in the several design departments of which he was head, completed about 40 aircraft projects between 1924 and

Nikolay Nikolayevich Polikarpov (centre) with his co-workers.

the end of 1928 and, even though few were actually built, his prestige was greatly enhanced by this fecundity. Such was his esteem that he was permitted to visit Britain, France, Germany and Holland to study the methodology of their aircraft industries.

To accelerate development work *zavod* 25 was set up at Khodynka to accommodate OPO-1 and provide it with a dedicated production facility. Polikarpov brought in his team on 24th February 1928 and in addition was appointed Deputy Director of the factory. (By then aircraft plants were no longer called GAZ but had been renumbered in 1927 into a list of defence plants; each was now called a *Gosudarstvennyy soyoooznyy zavod* ('state union factory', meaning that it had all-union, ie, national importance) or *zavod* for short.)

It was not long, however, before the fortunes of Polikarpov suffered a dramatic downturn. In September 1929 he was arrested, falsely accused of being an industrial saboteur and sentenced to death as an 'enemy of the people'. Fortunately, the sentence was commuted to 10 years imprisonment in a labour camp. Several other famous aircraft designers were similarly penalised; in 1937 even Andrey N. Tupolev suffered a similar fate. In December 1929 a group of engineers, including Polikarpov, was gathered together in Bootyrskaya prison, Moscow. There under the supervision of Goriyanov of the Main Political Directorate (OGPU), the forerunner of the infamous KGB, they were set to work to design aircraft, with Grigorovich as chief designer. This was subsequently discovered to be a blatant attempt by the OGPU to show that repression was the best form of motivation and therefore the most effective way to expand and control the industry. KB 'VT' (*konstrooktorskoye byuro 'Vnootrenn'aya tyur'ma'*, Internal Prison Design Bureau) was the name given to the new team.

More congenial accommodation was supplied in early 1930 when KB 'VT' moved to the grounds of *zavod* 39, also located in the Khodynka area. At first the team was led by Grigorovich but he was soon obliged to relinquish his role to Polikarpov whose fighter project, the future I-5 (I = *istrebitel'* – fighter), had been preferred over a Grigorovich design.

Further wholesale reorganisation took place on 3rd March 1930 when most defence trusts were replaced by 'All-Union Associations', one of which, the VAO (*Vsesoyooznoye aviatsionnoye ob"yedineniye*), was devoted to aircraft production. Aviatrest was part of VAO until 16th April of the same year when it was abolished. Around this time TsKB Aviatresta was reorganised into TsKB VAO at *zavod* 39, followed by the absorption of *zavod* 25 by *zavod* 39 in August 1930. Soon after, in September 1930, KB 'VT' became part of TsKB VAO but remained under OGPU control.

A change of fortune for Polikarpov occurred in June 1931 when Stalin was favourably impressed by the performance of the I-5 and observations that Polikarpov made at the Aviation Review which took place at the Central Airfield at Khodynka. Subsequently, on 7th July 1931 Polikarpov and some of his colleagues were granted an amnesty which allowed them their freedom, but the 'guilty' verdicts were not quashed until 1st September 1956, after the death of Stalin, by which time it was too late to benefit Polikarpov who had died of cancer on 30th July 1944.

The expansion of the aircraft industry also led to a steady increase in the number of experimental departments at TsKB VAO, each of which had a design team. There were ten of them by September 1931 when TsAGI (*Tsentrahl'nyy aero-ghidrodinamicheskiy institoot*, Central Aero- and Hydrodynamics Institute) took control of TsKB VAO and merged it with its own design team, AGOS (*aviahtsiya, ghidroaviahtsiya i opytnoe stroitel'stvo* – aircraft, seaplanes and experimental construction). This necessitated a move for the design teams to the TsAGI building in Moscow with *zavod* 39 being used as an experimental plant.

Within TsKB TsAGI, a design team was now known as a 'brigade' and Polikarpov was given charge of Brigade 3. However, he lost the post when he refused A. N. Tupolev's request to design all-metal aircraft, no doubt because of his predilection for the more abundant wood. As a result of this demotion Brigade 4 was absorbed by No. 3 where Polikarpov continued to work for a while as Pavel O. Sukhoi's deputy. It was decided that to achieve the objective of designing two fighters, the I-13 biplane with an M-32 engine and the I-14 monoplane with an M-38 engine, by mid-1933 two brigades were required and Polikarpov was appointed head of Brigade 5 tasked with developing the biplane fighter.

A further reorganisation had taken place in January 1933 in which the TsKB, now back at *zavod* 39, was separated from TsAGI and for this reason it was frequently referred to as TsKB-39 rather than its official title of TsKB GUAP. (GUAP, *Glahvnoye oopravleniye aviatsionnoy promyshlennosti*, Main Directorate of the Aviation Industry, had replaced VAO in early 1933.) Sergey V. Il'yushin was appointed to the new post of Chief Designer of TsKB GUAP and Deputy Director at *zavod* 39; in this capacity he managed five airframe and two aircraft equipment brigades. Polikarpov was put in charge of Brigade 3 specialising in the design and manufacture of fighter prototypes.

At a conference of the aviation industry and its customers in August 1935 Polikarpov was warmly congratulated on his fighter designs and took advantage of the occasion to express concern not only over the physical separation of design offices from the series production plants but also over the lamentable lack of modern experimental facilities. As a result of these comments it was decided to base as many design teams as possible in series production plants and to give each team its own experimental facilities. Thus aircraft design was decentralised in 1936 with the formation of OKBs (*opytno-konstrooktorskoye byuro*) – Experimental Design Bureaux based at production aircraft factories. The intention was that OKBs should compete in the development of aircraft and the winner would be mass-produced at the OKB's base factory. Thus the factory would have a strong incentive to co-operate with the OKB. Such was the prestige of Polikarpov, by now called 'the King of Fighters', that he was appointed Chief Designer of two OKBs, at plants No. 21 in Gor'kiy (now renamed back to Nizhniy Novgorod) and No. 84, then located in Khimki north of Moscow.

In December 1937 Polikarpov and his OKB were transferred to *zavod* 156, the base for the Tupolev OKB. After reviewing a range of projects with over-optimistic performance estimates he settled down to build the I-153 biplane and then the I-180 monoplane fighter. Sadly, the first prototype I-180 crashed on 15th December 1938, killing the famous test pilot Valeriy P. Chkalov. As soon as it was established that the accident was not attributable to a design fault, Polikarpov was allowed to build a second prototype; however, now Polikarpov's star was on the wane and a new generation of fighter designers headed by Aleksandr S. Yakovlev was exciting attention. After a visit to Germany Polikarpov returned to find that a second design group under Artyom I. Mikoyan had been formed at *zavod* 1. To add insult to injury it had taken over development of the I-400 (the future MiG-1), a design initiated by Polikarpov. Unable to reclaim his progeny and having lost 80 of his design staff to the new team, Polikarpov moved in July 1940 to *zavod* 51 as Director and Chief Designer.

When the German invasion necessitated evacuation to Novosibirsk, the OKB continued intensively drawing up fighter designs, including the I-185. Work on the I-185 continued after the return to *zavod* 51 in July 1943 but, regrettably, the fighter was rejected. Although terminally ill, Nikolai Polikarpov, with unflagging enthusiasm, worked on many new designs until his last days.

Acknowledgements

The authors wish to thank Ivan Rodionov, Mikhail Maslov, Lennart Andersson, Alexander Boyd and, as always, Nigel Eastaway (RART) for supplying materials used in this book; Peter Davison for the excellent photo gracing the back cover (top); and Dmitriy Komissarov for his aid with the manuscript.

Chapter 1

Early Endeavours

First Failures and First Success

2I-1N two-seat fighter

Polikarpov's first biplane fighter carried the designation 2I-N1 – ie, two-seat fighter with a single Napier engine (I stood for *istrebitel'* and N for Napier). Design work started in October 1924 at *zavod* 1 on this two-seat escort fighter which would also perform reconnaissance missions. This was the first Soviet two-seat fighter of indigenous design. It was to be powered by a 450-hp (336-kW) Napier Lion in-line engine which was covered by a neat metal cowling with the radiator under the lower wing leading edge. The wings were arranged as a single-bay sesquiplane and it had a semi-monocoque fuselage of oval section designed by Vladimir Denisov and constructed from glued layers of veneered wooden sheets (*shpon*) of 4 mm (0.16 in.) thickness in the forward section tapering to 2 mm (0.08 in.) at the tail. A skin of 1.5-mm (0.06-in.) plywood covered the wings and instead of internal bracing wires the wings had 3 mm (0.12 in.) thick plywood ribs and multiple 10 x 10 mm (0.4 x 0.4 in.) stringers. The upper wings had two spars but the shorter lower wings were of single-spar design. *Kol'chugalyuminiy* alloy V-struts separated the wings with the addition of external steel bracing wires. Two struts on each side of the fuselage also supported the upper wings. An aerofoil was fitted to the main fixed undercarriage axle and a small ski was used as a

tailskid. The armament comprised a forward-firing belt-fed synchronised 7.62-mm (.30 calibre) PV-1 machine-gun (*poolemyot vozdooshnyy*, = machine-gun for aircraft) and a similar calibre DA machine-gun ([*poolemyot*] *Degtyaryova aviatsionnyy*, Degtyaryov machine-gun for aircraft), ring-mounted in the rear cockpit. The 2I-N1 was not only a handsome machine but also one which was technically advanced for its time.

On 12th January 1926 the successful first flight took place and Polikarpov himself was in the rear cockpit for the fourth and eighth flights. However, during the ninth flight on 31st March 1926 the skin of the right upper wing ripped away at a height of 100 m (328 ft), resulting in the collapse of both wings on the right-hand side and the destruction of the aircraft in the subsequent crash. Tragically, the pilot, V. N. Filippov and the observer, V. V. Mikhaïlov, were both killed. Manufacturing defects were said to have been the cause; large portions of the wings' skin were found to have been badly glued and areas of rib caps and stringers had been assembled with no glue at all. Many panel pins were discovered to be unattached to the structure, and bradawl holes which should have been in the skin to equalise internal and external pressures had been omitted. As a result of the crash, which profoundly shocked the people

in the industry, there was a hiatus in aircraft design and subsequent over-reaction resulting in later aircraft such as the I-3, U-2, DI-2 and R-5 being over-strengthened and therefore heavier than necessary.

All further work on the 2I-N1 was cancelled, as was a projected single-seat variant, both because of the alleged unavailability of a suitable engine. Therefore only one prototype of the 2I-N1 was built.

Basic specifications of the 2I-N1

Span	12.0 m (39.38 ft)
Length	9.75 m (32.0 ft)
Wing area	27.15 m² (292 sq. ft)
Weight:	
empty	1,153 kg (2,542 lb)
loaded	1,700 kg (3,748 lb)
Fuel and oil weight	547 kg (1,205 lb)
Maximum speed	268 km/h (166.5 mph)
Climb to 1,000 m (3,280 ft)	1.8 minutes
Time to complete 360° circle	12 seconds
Service ceiling	7,100 m (23,300 ft)
Range	800 km (500 miles)
Landing speed, km/h (mph)	92 km/h (57 mph)

I-3 single-seat fighter

I-3 was the designation given to the next fighter to be built at GAZ-1 and designed at OSS

A three-quarters rear view of the ill-starred 2I-N1 fighter prototype. Note the shark fin-like shape of the vertical tail.

These three hitherto unpublished views of the 2I-N1 show well the extremely clean lines of Polikarpov's first fighter. Note how close the upper wings are mounted to the fuselage; the aircraft was obviously designed with a view to minimising drag.

under the supervision of Polikarpov. Delayed by investigations into the crash of the 2I-N1 and a determination for there to be no likelihood of a recurrence, work on this project was not started until mid-1926. This time the aircraft was a single-seat fighter, again with a sesquiplane and staggered wing formation. There was considerable discussion with Aviatrest on a suitable power plant. The question was whether to fit a liquid-cooled or an air-cooled engine. However, the subsequent first choice of a Wright Tornado III was vetoed by Polikarpov who argued convincingly that it did not generate sufficient power; accordingly the BMW VI liquid-cooled engine of 680 hp (507 kW) was accepted. It was also agreed that OSS, shortly (on 19th September 1926) to be reorganised as OPO-1 of TsKB Aviatresta, should design a radial engine version as soon as a suitable engine was available.

Archival sources differ as to whether the two prototypes were built at the experimental *zavod* 25 or series-production *zavod* 1, and the most likely explanation is that both factories were involved. *Zavod* 1 backed on to Khodynka airfield from which the prototypes made their first flight but *zavod* 25 was on the other side of the Leningradskiy Prospekt, a major road; therefore it is likely that most components were manufactured by *zavod* 25 but final assembly took place at *zavod* 1. Encouraged by the Soviet Air Force, preparations for starting series production began well in advance of official notification and two of the items so manufactured, the tail fin and rudder, later caused embarrassment when it was necessary to modify them.

On 14th May 1927, after a month's scrutiny of a wooden mock-up, approval of the design for the I-3 was given but only in principle and it was not until 3rd June 1927 that it was ratified formally by the NK VVS (*Narodnyy komissariaht Voyenno-vozdooshnykh sil* – People's Commissariat of the Air Force). Static tests started on a full-size model in October 1927. In the same month the agreement with BMW for manufacturing rights and technical assistance of the BMW VI engine was formalised. The first prototype was completed in early 1928 and made its maiden flight on 21st February with Mikhail M. Gromov at the controls. Factory trials lasted until 10th March and further tests at NII VVS (*Naoochno-issledovatel'skiy instittoot Voyenno-vozdooshnykh sil* – Research Institute of the Air Force) were completed by 14th April. On the whole the aircraft was liked, the main criticism being lack of directional stability at high speeds and a slight deficiency in control response between manoeuvres. The first difficulty was resolved by increasing the area of the vertical tail and installing horn balances on the elevators which were themselves given an increased angle of attack, and the second by the use of

A model of the I-3.

split ailerons. These modifications were introduced on the first batch of 79, although 40 of them had to manage with the smaller tail fin. Whether all modifications were fitted before delivery is not known but aircraft with construction numbers higher than 4026 certainly had the larger tail.

A second prototype I-3 was produced and flew for the first time in August 1928. It was then experimentally fitted with a propeller specially designed for high speed and this increased the top speed to 283 km/h (176 mph), albeit at the expense of a longer take-off run.

Although based on the design of the 2I-N1 with an oval-section semi-monocoque fuselage, the thickness of the glued veneered sheets was increased from 4 to 5 mm (0.16 to 0.2 in.) at the front, tapering to 3 mm (0.12 in.) at the tail, and the inside structure had four longerons and thirteen formers. Of note was the small headrest faired into the fuselage. Plywood and fabric were used to cover the wings which were given the Clark Y aerofoil profile with two box-type plywood spars having pine stringers and plywood caps. On this occasion internal bracing wires were fitted. All control surfaces consisted of a duralumin frame covered by fabric and all had cable controls except the elevators which had rods.

Ailerons were of a differential Frise-type design and the duralumin wing struts now had a back-to-front N-shape with a teardrop section and adjustable end-fittings and steel bracing wires. The main wheels were solid 750 x 125 mm (29.5 x 49.2 in.), later replaced by spoked 800 x 150 mm (31.5 x 5.9 in.) wheels; the undercarriage was pin-jointed, with rubber shock absorbers, and had a duralumin tailskid. Alternatively, skis of the type used on the R-1 could be fitted. The semi-retractable engine-cooling radiator extended below the fuselage immediately behind the aft undercarriage struts. Two fuel tanks were installed, the main one in the fuselage and a small 2.5-litre (0.55-gal.) tank, used for engine starting, in the upper wing centre section which also held an engine coolant tank.

Most series aircraft were fitted with the Soviet-built 680-hp (507-kW) M-17 engine, a licence-built version of the BMW VI but the first 39, like the prototypes, had genuine imported BMW VIs.

On the prototype and the 75 series-built aircraft the armament consisted of two synchronised Vickers machine-guns, to be replaced by the PV-1 7.62-mm type on subsequent aircraft. An OP-1 optical gunsight (*opticheskiy pritsel*) was used, centrally mounted with a KP-5 ring sight (*kol'tsevoy*

An early-production I-3 with the original small vertical tail undergoing manufacturer's flight tests.

Above: A late-production I-3 trestled during tests, probably for the purpose of boresighting the machine-guns. Compare the shape of the enlarged vertical tail to the example on the previous page.

Another early I-3 during tests. Note the water radiator enclosed by a heat-preserving cover and the lower part of the engine cowling removed, exposing the carburettor inlet.

pritsel) on the starboard side. A few of these aircraft had bomb racks to carry two 11.5-kg (25-lb) bombs. Production of the I-3 began in 1928 and a total of 389 or 399 (sources differ), including the aforementioned prototypes, were completed by the end of 1930.

Date	No. of aircraft built at *zavod* No. 1 *imeni Aviakhima*
1927	2 prototypes jointly with *zavod* No. 25
1928	35
1929	47
1930	250
1931	55

The above production table assumes a total of 389 were built. Known construction numbers are 3820 through 3857, 3915 through 4117, 4221 through 4253 and 4333 through 4356.

Basic specifications of the I-3

Span	11.0 m (36.1 ft)
Length	8.01 m (26.3 ft)
Wing area	27.85 m² (300 sq. ft)
Weight:	
empty	1,400 kg (3,086 lb)
loaded	1,846 kg (4,070 lb)
Weight of fuel	210 kg (462 lb)
Weight of oil	33 kg (73 lb)
Maximum speed at sea level	279 km/h (174 mph)
Climb to 1,000 m (3,280 ft)	1.8 minutes
Service ceiling	7,200 m (23,620 ft)
Range	585 km (364 miles)
Take-off run	150 m (241 ft)
Landing run	250 m (401 ft)
Landing speed	100 km/h (62 mph)

Operational history of the I-3

The I-3 commenced service with the VVS RKKA (*Voyenno-vozdooshnyye seely Raboche-krest'yahnskoy krahsnoy armii* – Air Force of the Workers' and Peasants' Red Army) in 1929 by replacing the Grigorovich I-2 in fighter units of the Belorussian Military District. The following units are known to have received them:

the 4th and 7th AE (*aviaeskadril'ya* – air squadron), later redesignated 106th and 107th IAE (*istrebitel'naya aviaeskadril'ya* – fighter squadron) respectively, at Smolensk;

the 13th and 5th AE (which later became the 108th and 7th IAE respectively) and the 9th AE at Bryansk;

the 17th and 19th AE, later called the 116th and 117th IAE respectively, were at unknown locations.

Deliveries to squadrons in the Ukraine started in 1930:

the 3rd AE (became the 109th IAE) and the 73rd *aviaotryad* (air detachment) at Kiev;

A Red Army Air Force pilot performs a pre-flight check on his I-3 which appears to have a striped spinner.

Red Army Air Force pilots pose beside a late-production I-3. Note the highly unusual rudder stripe which may be squadron markings.

Above: '7 Yellow', a standard I-3, in flight.

The DI-2 experimental two-seat derivative of the I-3.

weight reduction and greater strength looked set to replace the I-3's wooden structure and it was considered more prudent to start from scratch.

DI-2 two-seat fighter

The DI-2 or D-2 (*dvookhmesnyy istrebitel'*, two-seat fighter) was a two-seat derivative of the single seat I-3. Although most series-built I-3s were powered by the M-17 engine, an indigenous version of the BMW VI, the prototype had an imported motor. Design work was carried out in 1928 and the prototype was completed in 1929, making its first flight in early May.

The DI-2 differed from the I-3 in that it had a longer fuselage with an extra frame added to its centre section, an extended wingspan and enlarged rudder. For the gunner there were two 7.62-mm DA machine-guns on a Scarff ring mounted in the rear cockpit; these were in addition to the forward-firing pair. Test pilot Bukhgolts successfully completed factory trials but later in 1929 tailplane flutter in a dive caused the tail to break away and the aircraft crashed, tragically killing the pilot, A. V. Chekarev.

Only a single prototype was built; whether the reason for this was that Polikarpov was arrested in September 1929 is a matter for conjecture.

Basic specifications of the DI-2

Span	11.8 m (38.7 ft)
Length	8.2 m (26.9 ft)
Wing area	31.8 m² (342 sq. ft)
Weight:	
empty	1,557 kg (3,433 lb)
loaded	2,122 kg (4,678 lb)
Weight of fuel	210 kg (462 lb)
Weight of oil	33 kg (73 lb)
Maximum speed	256 km/h (159 mph)
Climb to 1,000 m (3,280 ft)	2.2 minutes
Service ceiling	6,300 m (20,670 ft)
Range	510 km (317 miles)
Time to complete 360° circle	14 seconds
Take-off run	180 m (590 ft)
Landing run	250 m (820 ft)
Landing speed	100 km/h (62 mph)

the 91st AE, subsequently renamed 33rd IAE, at Bobruisk.

The 1st, 2nd and 3rd Schools of Military Pilots also had some I-3 aeroplanes on their inventories.

By 1st October 1930 there were 252 I-3 fighters in service; 12 months later this number had increased to 282 and by 1st January 1932 to 297, from which total it fell to 249 on 1st January 1933 and to 239 towards the end of that year. It was finally retired from frontline fighter units in 1935, replaced by other Polikarpov fighters – the I-5, the I-15*bis* and

the much more advanced I-16. The main criticism from service pilots of the I-3 was that the plane sacrificed manoeuvrability for speed; a lament to be later repeated against the new generation of monoplane fighters.

No efforts were made to develop the I-3 by, for example, the fitting of a more powerful engine. One reason suggested for this omission is that after the arrest of Polikarpov in September 1929 there was an unwillingness to be associated with his products. A more cogent reason was that the introduction of the steel-framed fuselage with its attendant

In order to achieve better performance and manoeuvrability than that of the I-3 it was clear to Polikarpov that not only must more powerful engines be fitted but also the weight of the aircraft must be reduced. Only in this way could a fighter be built that would outclass its foreign rivals. At the Technical Council of Aviatrest meeting that took place on 10th August 1927 Polikarpov was able to persuade its members to accept his recommendations and in September he was asked to start work on the new fighter which ultimately became the I-5. At another Council meeting on 21st

September Andrei N.Tupolev, the influential head of AGOS and Deputy Director of TsAGI, took the decision to pass over Polikarpov and give this task to Pavel O.Sukhoi whose section, under Tupolev's supervision, had designed the successful I-4 fighter.

After taking part in the 4th International Aviation Exhibition in February 1928 Polikarpov returned home to become Chief Designer and Deputy Director of a factory, *zavod* 25, which had been specially equipped to build experimental aircraft. One of his first projects there was to design a high-speed fighter developed from the I-3 but fitted with a radial engine. This was to become the I-6

I-6 (*izdeliye* 29) single-seat fighter

Polikarpov was assigned the design of the I-6 fighter, alias *izdeliye* 29, plans for which had been incorporated into the experimental aircraft section of the Five-Year Plan formulated in 1928. (*Izdeliye* (product) such-and-such was a common term used for Soviet/Russian military hardware items in paperwork.) Strict orders were given that it must be delivered by 1st August 1929. Work on its design started in September 1928.

The OSS (later called OPO-1) of TsKB Aviatresta originally envisaged the I-6 as the radial-engined fighter to be compared with the in-line engined I-3, but time had moved on and it was decided that a more relevant comparison would be between two radial-engined fighters, one of traditional wooden monocoque construction and the other with a metal-framed mixed-construction fuselage. The engine chosen was the 480-hp (358-kW) Bristol Jupiter VI for which a contract for licence production had been negotiated. Polikarpov was determined to build this aircraft with the lowest possible weight and was helped in this respect by installing an air-cooled engine which was shorter than the BMW VI powering the I-3 and required neither coolant nor radiators. Once again the semi-monocoque fuselage was constructed from glued layers of shpon 5 mm (0.2 in.) thick at the front, as on the I-3, but tapering to only 2.5 mm (0.1 in.) at the tail. The wings and interplane struts were of a similar design and structure to those of the I-3. The result was that the I-6 had an empty weight that was only 62% of that of the I-3. The wooden propeller was given a spinner and the duralumin helmeted cowls of the engine's cylinders left open at the front and top to facilitate cooling.

As a result of Polikarpov's arrest and imprisonment in September 1929 the tempo of the project inevitably slowed to a snail's pace and the maiden flight of the first prototype did not take place until 30th March 1930. The second prototype followed shortly after and both were displayed at that year's May Day Parade. It is likely that the two aircraft

A group of pilots poses in front of an I-3 with the tail number '1 Red'. This aircraft is unusual in having common exhaust manifolds instead of the standard individual exhaust stubs.

were first equipped with imported 480-hp (358-kW) Bristol Jupiter VI engines but these were subsequently replaced by the licence-built version designated M-22.

On 13 June 1930 one I-6 crashed after the test pilot baled out; a measure which, in the opinion of the Soviet aviation historian Vadim B. Shavrov, was without justification. After 12 months' deliberation comparing the I-6 with the outwardly similar (but structurally different) I-5, designed by Polikarpov's 'internal prison' team, the authorities finally decided that it was to be the I-5 which would be forwarded to series production. There was very little to choose between them on performance criteria, with the exception of rate of turn where the prototypes of the I-5 could complete a 360° turn in 9.5 seconds whereas the I-6 took 15 seconds. The most likely reason for the choice was the stronger structure of the I-5 but some influence was probably exerted by the intention to fit series-built aircraft with the heavier armament of four machine-guns. Strange to relate, Polikarpov was not informed of all the test results of the

I-6 until he was released from the 'internal prison' in 1933.

Only two prototypes of the I-6 were built.

Basic specifications of the I-6

Span:	
upper wings	9.7 m (31.8 ft)
lower wings	7.5 m (24.6 ft)
Length	6.8 m (22.3 ft)
Wing area	20.5 m² (221 sq. ft)
Weight:	
empty	868 kg (1,914 lb)
loaded	1,280 kg (2,822 lb)
Maximum speed	280 km/h (174 mph)
Climb to 1,000 m (3,280 ft)	1.5 minutes
Service ceiling	7,500 m (24,600 ft)
Range	700 km (435 miles)
Time to complete 360° circle	15 seconds
Take-off run	90 m (295 ft)
Landing run	200 m (656 ft)
Landing speed	95 km/h (59 mph)

One of the I-6 fighter prototypes.

Above: Production I-3s lined up at an airfield.

These I-3s sport white lightning bolts on the fuselage (probably as unit markings). The engine cowlings were invariably left unpainted.

Chapter 2

I-5: Born in Prison

I-5 single-seat fighter

Before any decision was taken as to which fighter should succeed the I-3 on the production lines it was decided in the 1928 Experimental Aircraft Plan to build the I-5 with a radial engine and mixed wood and metal construction for comparison with the all-wood I-6. Whilst speed was a major consideration, there were two other factors for the designers to take into account; the first was to maximise manoeuvrability and the second, to ensure the fighter's adaptability to mass production methods. The original instructions stipulated that the I-6 prototype be ready by 1st August and the I-5 by 1st September 1929 but neither of these deadlines was met. This double failure may have provided the excuse for the OGPU to incarcerate Polikarpov on grounds of industrial sabotage rather than to attribute it to inefficiency.

Design work on what was to become the I-5 had been started by Pavel O. Sukhoi under the supervision of Andrey N. Tupolev at AGOS where the prototype was to have been designated ANT-12, the letters being Tupolev's initials. The formation of 'internal prison' design teams by the OGPU meant that someone more powerful even than Tupolev was now influencing the choice of chief designer. It is not known for certain why the internal prison design bureau (KB 'VT') and not AGOS was finally given the job of designing the I-5 but the most plausible explanation for this decision is the influence of the OGPU. An alternative suggestion was that Tupolev preferred to concentrate on the development of heavy bombers and did not press the case for AGOS to keep the I-5 project. At the KB 'VT' Dmitriy P. Grigorovich was chosen as chief designer, but Polikarpov soon convinced Goriyanov of the OGPU, who was nominally in charge of the KB, that his fighter concept was superior to that of Grigorovich. Polikarpov was accordingly placed in charge of the design team which in early 1930 moved to hangar No. 7 at *zavod* 39.

The full-scale mock-up was approved on 28th March 1930. Just a month later the first prototype, designated VT-11, was completed and delivered to Moscow's Central Airfield (Khodynka) for testing.

It was a single-bay sesquiplane powered by an imported 450-hp (336-kW) supercharged Bristol Jupiter VII engine with a hel-

Known as the VT-11, the first prototype of the I-5 had a red and silver colour scheme. Note the VT logo superimposed on the red star on the tail, denoting *vnootrenn'aya tyur'ma* (internal prison).

meted cowl and a 2.9-m (9.5-ft) propeller. The aircraft exterior was finished in silver dope with a red cheat line and adorned by a red 'VT' logo inserted in the red star on the rudder. Its first flight took place on 29th April 1930 with V. L. Bukhgol'ts at the controls.

A second prototype, known as VT-12, was built with an unsupercharged Bristol Jupiter VI engine, larger rubber shock absorbers on the main undercarriage legs and a shorter vertical tail with a more rounded top. The aircraft was doped green, with the dedication 'Klim Voroshilov' emblazoned in large white letters on the sides of the fuselage.

Both these prototypes had large spinners and each engine cylinder head was fully covered by a helmet-cowling but the third prototype, aircraft VT-13, which first flew on 1st July 1930 had no spinner and a NACA cowling fully covering the cylinder heads of a locally manufactured 600-hp (448-kW) M-15 engine. Radiator slats gave improved cooling and the rear fuselage from behind the cockpit was built up to enhance the aerodynamics and give the pilot better protection. This latest aircraft was again doped silver with a red rudder and was given a large red pennant bearing the dedication *'Podarok shesnadtsatomu Parts"yezdu'* (A gift to the 16th Congress of the [Communist] Party). Such 'gifts' were common practice in the Soviet Union.

During the month between 13th July and 13th August 1931 the second prototype successfully underwent its State Acceptance Trials and on 13th September 1931 was formally ordered into production at *zavod* No. 21 named after Sergo Ordzhonikidze in Gor'kiy and *zavod* 1 at Khodynka. Preparations for production, such as the ordering of machine tools and components, were already well in hand but it was some time from the start of manufacture before an acceptable standard of finished product was achieved. The first production aircraft were used for in-service evaluation by the VVS and by 1st October 1931 54 I-5 fighters had been delivered. *Zavod* 21 had not been open for very long and its inexperience presented many problems. In particular, its inability to make a consistently standard product resulted in a lower performance for its I-5s than that of the prototypes. This shortcoming was a direct consequence of the factory's inability to maintain a consistently low airframe weight. All series production aircraft from *zavod* 21 were built with 480-hp (358-kW) M-22 engines and Townend rings, but some imported Jupiter VI engines were installed on early models from *zavod* 1 before it changed to the M-22.

It was intended to build the I-5 at *zavod* 135 in Khar'kov, this time with M-15 engines but none were actually built. No reason was

Above: Another view of the VT-11.

A mechanic cranks up the M-22 engine of a red/silver dope I-5 flown by Russian Civil War hero I. U. Pavlov; note the compressed air bottle for engine starting. The legend on the fuselage reads *Za VKP(b)* (For the All-Union Communist Party (Bol'sheviks)); the rudder has a downward-pointing curved white arrow.

Above: The green-painted second prototype I-5 designated VT-12 and emblazoned 'Klim Voroshilov'. Initially the pilot had to do without a headrest. Note the difference in the shape of the rudder as compared to the VT-11 and the bigger shock absorbers.

Another view of the VT-12 following modifications, including the fitment of a faired headrest. All three prototypes, as well as the aircraft of the pre-production batch, were powered by Bristol Jupiter engines and featured this characteristic cowling design.

A pre-production I-5, likewise powered by a Bristol Jupiter VI.

ever given but speculation connects it with the decision of the VVS not to use the unreliable M-15.

Meanwhile *zavod* 39, having absorbed *zavod* 25 in August 1930, had assembled about ten pre-production I-5s between August and October and was striving to improve the design, a process that continued throughout the production run. For example, the following alterations were made: cooling vents were introduced into the crankcase fairing; a stronger tailskid was fitted; a pitot tube and static vent were installed on the starboard upper wing; a faired headrest was provided for the pilot; the undercarriage was strengthened and a duralumin propeller with ground-adjustable pitch replaced the original fixed-pitch wooden airscrew. Some aircraft were also fitted with wheel spats. All pre-production I-5s had Jupiter VI engines. These modifications were consolidated into what was intended to be the standard 1933 model (referred to by some sources as the I-5*bis*). The overall effect was to increase the top speed at sea level by 17.5 km/h (11 mph) over that of the second prototype but this advantage deteriorated with altitude until at 5,000 m (16,400 ft) the fighter was slightly slower. It was unfortunate that the improvements had increased the total weight, thus degrading the rate of climb and service ceiling. Nonetheless, most of these modifications were implemented as the unofficial 1933 production standard at *zavod* 21 by the middle of the year, even though two attempts to get them all approved as the official standard failed.

A side view of the same aircraft during trials. Note the spoked wheels without covers and the lack of national insignia.

Above: A Jupiter-powered I-5 suspended from the cable of a crane.

This view of an I-5 in the final assembly shop with the wing skins still to be fitted illustrates the wing structure well. Note the short headrest fairing characteristic of the initial production aircraft.

Above: A well-weathered production I-5 powered by an M-22 engine with a Townend ring and a metal propeller.

Many early M-22 powered I-5s, like this one, had wooden propellers with small spinners.

Three views of the I-15 *etalon* (production standard-setter) for 1933, showing the wheel spats, metal propeller, longer headrest fairing and aerial mast.

Above and below: Close-up of the cowling on an M-22 powered I-5 with metal prop. Note the different size of the cooling apertures in the crankcase fairing

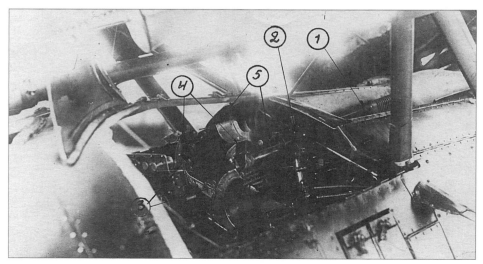

Close-up of the centre fuselage, showing the windshield, the OP-1 optical gunsight, the cabane struts and the breeches of the upper machine-guns.

One fault noted in the State Acceptance Trials was the tendency of the aircraft to execute an uncontrolled 180° turn when landing in light wind conditions. Compensating with rudder movement broke the outer wheel on the turn, causing the fighter to stand on its nose or flip over. Even experienced pilots, such as the Commander-in-Chief of the VVS Yakov I. Alksnis, experienced this problem. I. F. Petrov, an engineer from NII VVS, suggested shortening the undercarriage by 15 cm (5.9 in.) and positioning it 12 cm (4.75 in.) further forward. This was tried and found to be effective, as Alksnis himself confirmed. All existing and future production aircraft were given this undercarriage design and Petrov was awarded the Order of the Red Star for his ingenuity.

In the expectation of improving manoeuvrability a small number of aircraft had experimental streamlined leading wing struts which swivelled about their vertical axis in conjunction with rudder movement. This was not a success.

To reduce the number of accidents that had resulted from pilots being unable to control a spinning aircraft a spin test programme was carried out at NII VVS. Test pilots Piotr M. Stefanovsky, A. I. Filin and P. M. Stepanchonok were involved and it was during this programme that Stepanchonok was forced to bale out when he lost control in an inverted spin. It was as a direct consequence of the bravery of the test pilots that a set of safe spin recovery procedures could be issued. An interesting sequel was the formation of the first Soviet aerobatic demonstration team under the leadership of Stepanchonok.

Structural description of the series-built I-5

The I-5 was a single-seat single-bay biplane with staggered wings of sesquiplane format. Internally the fuselage had a gas-welded tubular steel structure and internal bracing wires, having four longerons with stringers to give the fuselage covering a streamlined shape. Light duralumin panels about 0.6 mm (0.02 in.) thick covered the forward fuselage as far back as the rear of the cockpit. The aft fuselage was fabric-covered, with duralumin panels positioned below the tailplane to allow easy access to the tailskid shock absorber.

All the fuselage duralumin panels were made detachable by affixing them to the frame with spring-loaded fasteners and steel pins. Lacing secured the fabric skin and seams were covered with calico strips. Behind the engine, a fireproof bulkhead protected the 165-litre (36 Imp. gal.) fuel tank. A fire extinguisher was installed with outlets to the petrol pump, inlet pipe and carburettor. A corrugated duralumin frame supported the pilot's seat, his parachute acting as a cushion. The windscreen was of thick celluloid.

The wings were constructed with two spars. The upper wings were built in three sections (a centre section and two outer panels); each lower wing was a one-piece panel attached directly to the side of the fuselage. A Goettingen-436 aerofoil section was used. The spars were separated by a width equal to half the chord. The duralumin interwing struts and steel bracing wires were similar to the I-6, with the struts having the now familiar 'reversed N' shape. The same strut formation was used to connect the upper wings to the fuselage. Twenty ribs were used in the upper wings and fifteen in the lower. Ailerons were only fitted to the upper wings, each attached by a set of three bracketed hinges. The wing spars and ribs were wooden. As on the fuselage, laced lacquered fabric, with the seams protected by calico strips, covered the empennage and wings, except for the roots of the lower wings which were covered in plywood. All wing leading edges were sheathed in duralumin for the first 150 cm (59 in.). To provide a better view for the pilot the centre section trailing edge was severely cut back and the leading edge given similar but much less drastic treatment.

The tail surfaces had a duralumin framework covered with doped fabric and joints at the junction of the tail unit with the fuselage were covered by duralumin fairings. The control surfaces had horn balances. The horizontal tail was offset 3.5 mm (0.14 in.) to port to compensate for the engine's torque but could be adjusted when on the ground. Bracing wires above and below the horizontal tail were used on the prototypes but on series aircraft a strut on each side replaced the lower wires.

Aircraft from the earlier batches had fixed tailskids but later versions had smaller skids synchronised to move with the rudder. The compression shock absorbers of the main undercarriage were constructed of 16 pieces of rubber each 20 mm (0.8 in.) thick separated by steel rings. A one-piece axle joined the wheels. Some aircraft had streamlined teardrop-shaped wheel fairings. All the prototypes as well as the aircraft involved in the 'Zveno' parasite aircraft experiments had longer mainwheel legs and smaller diameter but wider tyres of 750 x 125 mm (29.5 x 4.9 in.) compared with the standard 760 x 100 mm (30 x 3.9 in.). Skis could be fitted for winter conditions.

Some of the early aircraft had imported Bristol Jupiter VI engines but the M-22, a developed license-built version, was used in the others. Both developed 480 hp and were optimised for low altitudes. Almost all series aircraft had a Townend ring cowl, a duralumin 2.7-m (8.9-ft) propeller with ground-adjustable pitch and no spinner. However, early batches had fixed-pitch wooden propellers of 2.9 m (9.5 ft) diameter, some with a metal boss.

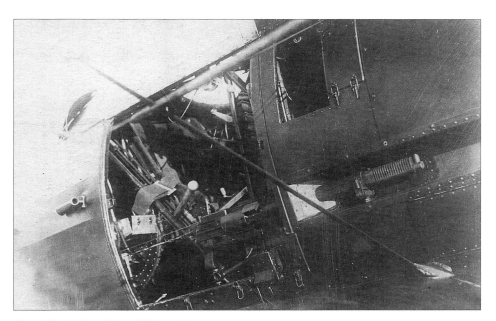
Above: The starboard lower PV-1 machine-gun.

Above: The port side of the cockpit on a standard production I-5.

The starboard side of the cockpit with the metal skin panels removed.

An I-5 on the the starboard wing of a Tupolev TB-3 bomber modified into the *Zveno-2* composite aircraft, seen from the bomber's dorsal gunner's station. The *Zveno-2* included three I-5 'parasite fighters' carried atop the wings and fuselage.

The gun armament initially comprised two 7.62-mm (.30 calibre) PV-1 machine-guns equipped with a PUL-9 synchroniser, with 600 rounds per gun, but it was hoped to change this on series-produced aircraft to four guns, two each side of the fuselage, with a total of 2,400 rounds and an OP-1 telescopic sight. Unfortunately the weight of production aeroplanes was greater than expected and very few received four machine-guns. Der-5 underwing bomb racks ('Der' is an abbreviation of *derzhahtel'*, holder) could be fitted to carry two 10-kg (22-lb) bombs in overload configuration.

Comparisons drawn up by the VVS of the I-5 and contemporary foreign fighters showed it to be lighter than the Bristol Bulldog, Curtiss P-6E and Heinkel He 37 and superior to them in rate of climb and manoeuvrability in the horizontal plane but it had a lower top speed. Its performance in simulated dogfights with available foreign fighters at NII VVS convinced the Soviet authorities of the I-5's superiority at medium altitudes. The I-5 stayed in the service of the VVS until 1942, although long before the war started the type had been relegated to the advanced trainer role.

Production of the I-5, excluding three prototypes and about ten development aircraft built at *zavod* 39, totalled 803 and was distributed as follows:

Number of aircraft built at:

	zavod 1 imeni Aviakhima	zavod 21 imeni Ordzhonikidze
1931	66	-
1932	76	10
1933	-	321
1934	-	330
Total	142	661

It is worth noting that between late 1932 and the end of 1933 *zavod* 1, after stopping production of the I-5, built 131 I-7 fighters (Heinkel He 37c manufactured under licence). This could be taken as an indication that the Soviet Air Force was covering itself against uncertainties about the I-5's performance. Although it transpired that their doubts were unfounded, the decision to continue producing the German design was justified by the alleged superiority of the I-7 at low altitudes. On the other hand, Polikarpov's I-16 monoplane fighter, a much more logical decision, replaced the I-5 on the production lines of *zavod* 21.

The figures given in the following table are those of a typical I-5 series production machine:

Basic specifications of the I-5

Span:	
upper wings	10.24 m (33.6 ft)
lower wings	7.4 m (24.3 ft)
Length	6.78 m (22.2 ft)
Wing area	21.3 m² (229 sq. ft)
Weight:	
empty	934 kg (2,079 lb)
loaded	1,355 kg (2,987 lb)
Fuel weight	180 kg (397 lb)
Maximum speed at sea level	278 km/h (173 mph)
Climb to 1,000 m (3,280 ft)	1.6 minutes
Service ceiling	7,500 m (24,600 ft)
Range	660 km (410 miles)
Time to complete 360° circle	10 seconds
Take-off run	100 m (328 ft)
Landing run	200 m (656 ft)
Landing speed	95 km/h (59 mph)

Operational history of the I-5

New aircraft deliveries to the VVS started in late 1931 and by the time that 1932 drew to a close the I-5 comprised 20% of its fighter force, a percentage which grew to 40% by the end of 1933, making the I-5 the most numerous fighter then in service. The Leningrad, Ukraine and Trans-Baikal Military Districts were the first to receive them, followed shortly after by the Far East, Belorussian and Moscow Military Districts. The resources of the last

Above: Seen from the bomber's cockpit, the portside I-5 of the *Zveno-2* is just about to separate from the TB-3. Note the tail support strut falling away into the folded position.

An I-5 on the centreline station of the *Zveno-2* composite aircraft. Note the trough-like structures restraining the fighter's wheels; the mother ship's twin cockpit windshields are just visible beyond them.

Above: A Jupiter-engined I-5 carrying two 50-kg (110-lb) bombs, most likely during weapons trials. The lack of the spinner is noteworthy.

Above and below: I-5 '2 Red' was equipped experimentally with triple launchers for 82-mm unguided rockets. It is seen here trestled for ground trials of the system.

mentioned were strengthened in 1933 when the 10th IAB (*istrebitel'naya aviabri-gahda* – Fighter Brigade) based at Lyubertsy and Ivanovo began re-equipping with the I-5. By the end of 1934 most of the I-3 and I-4 fighters in the VVS had been replaced and deliveries of the I-5 had commenced to units of the VMF (*Voyenno-morskoy flot*, Navy).

The I-5 was a demanding aeroplane to fly, and there were other peculiarities into the bargain. This is how the late Mark L. Gallai, the famous Soviet test pilot, described it in his book *My Flight Log*:

'*After flying it I was convinced that the I-5 is quite a handful, a capricious aircraft. However, if you are careful with the controls and do not offend the machine with rough actions, it will not depart from controlled flight. What annoyed me a lot more was the absolutely revolting smell it emitted. The M-22 engine was lubricated with castor oil. I hope you never had to smell burnt castor oil... During my long aviation career I never had a more disgusting job than to scrape off dead locusts that had become stuck to the underside of the I-5's wings. Locust fried in castor oil sure is a dish to make you faint.*'

Many new and innovative weapons were tested, using the I-5 as a carrier. Small 8-kg (17.6-lb) anti-aircraft bombs were dropped on a towed target drogue by an I-5 of the 5th IAB in Kiev during the summer of 1934. A primitive unguided rocket known as the **Fleyta** (Flute) was carried in clusters of five under each lower wing of an I-5 and test-fired. Another interesting experiment was the ground testing of 82-mm (3.2-in.) RS-82 rockets (*raketnyy snaryad* – rocket projectile) fired from a triple underwing launcher attached to both inner and outer portions of the lower wings with the aircraft securely attached to a firm base. In this way the accuracy of the rocket could be accurately assessed. Later, six rockets were fired at both aerial and ground targets from each of two airborne I-5s. Altogether 692 RS-82 rockets were expended in these trials and the weapon was used successfully in World War Two.

Aircraft development accelerated during the 1930s and the realization of how far it had advanced in Western Europe was brought home to the Soviets in the summer of 1934 during a visit by Pierre Cotte, the French Minister for Aviation. After his arrival at Kiev in a Caudron C.635 Simoun four-seat monoplane he was given an honorary escort of I-5 fighters for the next leg of his journey. Unfortunately the escorting I-5s were not fast enough to keep up with the Simoun and were compelled to turn back.

Aggressive Japanese tactics in Mongolia during 1937 resulted in squadron number 21, with both interceptor and ground attack flights, being deployed to Tamar-Bulak for border patrols. This apparent show of strength did not deter the Japanese because they had on hand a strong force of Kawasaki Ki-10, Army Type 92 biplanes and Nakajima Army Type 91 parasol monoplanes. No evidence of confrontation between these types of Soviet and Japanese aeroplanes has been found, which was opportune because the Japanese biplane was more manoeuvrable than the I-5 and their monoplane faster.

When Vladimir S. Vakhmistrov started his *Zveno* (flight, as a tactical unit) experiments in 1933 the I-5 was involved. To protect long-range bombers from enemy fighters an I-4, later replaced by an I-5, was carried under each wing of a Tupolev TB-1 twin-engined bomber piloted by Piotr M. Stefanovskiy. Flying the parasite fighters were I. F. Grozd and Vladimir K. Kokkinaki. Further trials were conducted with Zveno-2, using the four-engined TB-3 with two I-5s on top of the wings and a third on the fuselage. At an air display which took place at Monino in November 1935, a six-aircraft Zveno was displayed: a TB-3 carried two I-5s on top of the wings, two I-16s underneath and a Grigorovich I-Z which flew onto an under-fuselage trapeze. All five fighters were then safely released. (Whilst this concept is basically flawed in that the extra drag of the 'parasites' reduced the speed of the escorted bomber force to an unacceptable level, it was successfully used for a low-level bombing attack by a combat unit known as Zveno-SPB in which a TB-3 carried two I-16 *tip* 5 fighters armed with bombs (these were known as SPB, *skorosnoy pikeeruyuschchiy bombardirovschchik* – fast dive-bomber). Its moment of glory was the destruction of a key railway bridge over the Danube at Chernovod, Romania, on 25th August 1941 and a number of other operations were also completed from bases in the Crimea.)

A fighter-bomber version of the I-5 was developed at Piotr I. Grokhovskiy's OKB. Beam-type bomb racks were designed for installation under the lower wings to carry two 250-kg (550-lb) bombs. One of the tests involved the aircraft diving down close to the target – the first time dive-bombing had been tried in the Soviet Union. Unfortunately the extra weight and drag of the bombs adversely affected performance to the extent that the I-5 fighter-bomber concept was rejected at the time, although it was resurrected during World War Two after the Luftwaffe had proved its effectiveness.

As new and more potent fighters such as the I-15 and I-16 entered service with the VVS, the I-5 was increasingly used as a fighter transition trainer; pupils starting on the Polikarpov U-2 moved on to the Yakovlev UT-2, followed by a stint on the I-5 before graduating to the I-15 or I-16. The Air Force Academy named after Nikolay Ye. Zhukovskiy received eight

A rare picture of an I-5 fitted with skis.

I-5s in 1933 but more were transferred to other flying schools in large numbers, starting in 1936 at Borisoglebsk and Kacha. By the end of 1937 all I-5 aircraft had been phased out of service with first-line units.

Enormous losses of aircraft in the opening attacks of the German invasion of the Soviet Union and later the disruption of aircraft production led to use of this obsolete fighter as a ground attack aircraft and night bomber. This would be the first time the type had been used in action. Many of the surviving I-5s were given an additional pair of machine-guns during the war as an alternative to carrying bombs. Possibly the most desperate time for the USSR was at the end of 1941 and the beginning of 1942 when the shortage of aircraft was so acute that almost anything that could fly was pressed into service and there are records of 605th and 606th IAPs (*istrebitel'nyye aviatsionnyye polki*, fighter regiments) using the I-5 on night bomber operations in the Battle for Moscow. Based at Bykovo, Pushkino and Klin, they continued in service until replaced by a more modern type in February 1942. In September 1941 the 2nd ShAP (*shtoormovoy aviatsionnyy polk* – attack air regiment) was formed from Crimean Front Air Force reserve personnel and equipped with 32 I-5s for ground attack. These aircraft were found in flying schools and returned to airworthy condition by the regiment for use in the Crimea, soldiering on until January 1942 when the regiment was withdrawn to Chapayevsk for conversion to the Il'yushin IL-2 and redesignated the 766th ShAP.

The Black Sea Fleet Air Arm used refurbished I-5 fighters and in November 1941 they represented half of its entire fighter inventory which in total was only 44. One regiment was the 11th ShAP commanded by Major I. M. Rassoodkov which covered the Red Army's retreat to Sevastopol'. Captain N. T. Khroostalyov led 20 I-5s in ground attacks against enemy troops and armour in the Bel'bek

Valley and deliberately dived his blazing plane onto them when it was certain that he could not avoid crashing.

Regrettably no I-5 fighters are still in existence, but a 3/4 scale replica powered by a 36-hp flat-twin engine from a Dnepr MT-10-36 motorcycle was built in 1989 by the Ivanovo-based company NPO Antares. It was shown at Moscow-Khodynka in August 1989 and in the static line at the 1993 Moscow Air Show. The aircraft is painted to represent the I-5 flown by Russian Civil War hero I. U. Pavlov.

I-5UTI fighter trainer

A two-seat dual-control trainer version designated I-5UTI (*oochebno-trenirovochnyy istrebitel'*, fighter trainer) was manufactured in small numbers at one of the factories. It is believed that about 20 were built. The cockpit of the I-5 was moved back and a second placed in front of it.

I-6 (the second aircraft to carry this designation)

This designation was reported to have been used in 1931 for a modified I-5 with an experimental propeller fabricated from a new material, no details of which were released. As the maximum speed was 20 km/h (12 mph) slower than the standard model, trials were soon abandoned.

I-13 single-seat fighter project

Whilst at TsKB TsAGI and working under Sukhoi in late 1931, Polikarpov was tasked with designing a sesquiplane fighter fitted with a water-cooled V-16 engine under development as the M-32. This agile fighter armed with four machine-guns was to be called I-13 and was tabled to be ready for evaluation in mid-1933. Problems persisted with the engine and the project was abandoned in 1932, much to Polikarpov's relief as he favoured using a Wright Cyclone radial engine

Above: This I-5 posing for an air-to-air shot wears an unusual two-tone version of the Soviet star insignia on the rudder.

ЛЕНИНГРАДСКОМУ
АЭРОКЛУБУ -
от ЦК ВЛКСМ
секр. ЦК

I-5s were operated not only by the Red Army Air Force but by air clubs as well. This example is a gift from the Central Committee of the Young Communist League to the Leningrad Air Club and is signed by the Central Committee Secretary.

Above: A Red Army Air Force I-5 pilot receives congratulations from his commander after a successful mission. Note the twin bomb racks under the lower wings and the unusual red stripe on the fin connected with the tail number '5 Red'.

Another typical publicity shot: a fighter pilot puts on his flying gloves while watching for the signal to scramble. This I-5 has a black-painted Townend ring and a wooden propeller with metal leading edge sheaths.

Above: A still from a Soviet documentary showing a pair of I-5s in echelon starboard formation.

A trio of civil-registered I-5s takes off. No, they're not warbirds; the registrations in the SSSR-Sxxx series (the flight leader's aircraft is SSSR-S2570 and the second aircraft from camera is SSSR-S2590) indicate they are operated by Osoaviakhim, the organisation which controlled Soviet air clubs before World War Two. Note the white arrow on the rudder of SSSR-S2570.

Chapter 3

The Legendary Chato

I-14a single-seat fighter project

For some time Polikarpov had been considering a replacement for the I-5 in which his primary aim was to maximise manoeuvrability in line with the intention of the VVS to use a combination of highly agile biplanes and very fast monoplanes as fighters. At the suggestion of Sergey V. Il'yushin, Polikarpov's Brigade 5 started work on a radial-engined biplane fighter in July 1932. In December 1932 a mock-up and drawings were presented to the VVS and reviewed at the same time as Pavel O. Sukhoi's I-14 monoplane. Polikarpov's contribution was designated I-14a, a gull-winged single-bay radial-engined sesquiplane with streamlined single wing struts, an enclosed cockpit, a retractable undercarriage (the wheels retracting into the fuselage sides *à la* Grumman F2F or Brewster Buffalo) and a single-strutted horizontal tail. Both Polikarpov's and Sukhoi's designs were accepted for further development and to avoid confusion the I-14a was redesignated I-15.

I-15 (TsKB-3) single-seat fighter

On 13th January 1933 TsKB TsAGI was reorganised as TsKB GUAP (**Glav**noye **oopravleniye aviatsionnoy promysh**lennosti, Chief Directorate of the Aviation Industry) and the TsKB reported directly to the newly formed GUAP without TsAGI as an intermediary. At the head of TsKB GUAP was Sergey V. Il'yushin, which was good news for Polikarpov as he received appreciably more support from Il'yushin than he ever had from Tupolev. Design work for the I-15 was now at *zavod* 39 where Polikarpov's team was known as Brigade 2. I-15 was the service designation of this fighter but it was known to the design bureau as TsKB-3, denoting their third design. Confusion can arise because at a later date there was another TsKB-3; this time the title referred to a Third Central Design Bureau at Grivno dedicated to the development of cartridges. To cloud the issue further, there was also a contemporary TsKBS-3 in Leningrad developing heavy guns on rail-trucks!

The prototype TsKB-3 was completed in October 1933. It was finished in bright red, broken only on the rudder by a white circle containing a red star overwritten with the number '39' in black – a reference to its factory of origin (*zavod* 39). An imported Wright SGR-1820-F3 Cyclone engine was fitted, delivering 630 hp (470 kW) at sea level increasing to 715 hp (533 kW) at 2,000 m (6,500 ft). A single-bay strutted biplane, the TsKB-3 was of mixed wood and metal construction with the upper wings attached to the fuselage in a gull-type formation. This feature gave rise to the type's nickname of *Chaika* (Seagull). It was, however, not such an advanced design as the original I-14a mock-up; for example, the retractable undercarriage and enclosed cockpit were absent. One plausible explanation is that, as Polikarpov had also included these untried features on his I-16 monoplane fighter, he understandably did not want to take too many risks with both designs.

Valeriy P. Chkalov, who was very enthusiastic about the new fighter and particularly its incredible manoeuvrability, carried out the first flight and then factory evaluation tests from 18th November 1933. A new record was created when a 360° turn was completed in just over 8 seconds. These tests were successfully completed in only 26 days and a maximum speed of 350 km/h (217 mph) was achieved at 3,000 m (9,800 ft) but the prototype was damaged on 23rd November 1933,

The TsKB-3 prototype nearing completion in August-September 1933. With the fabric skin still to be fitted, the airframe structure is clearly visible; note that the rudder is still missing at this stage.

Above and below: The red-painted first prototype TsKB-3 on skis in front of the final assembly shop of the Moscow aircraft factory No. 39.

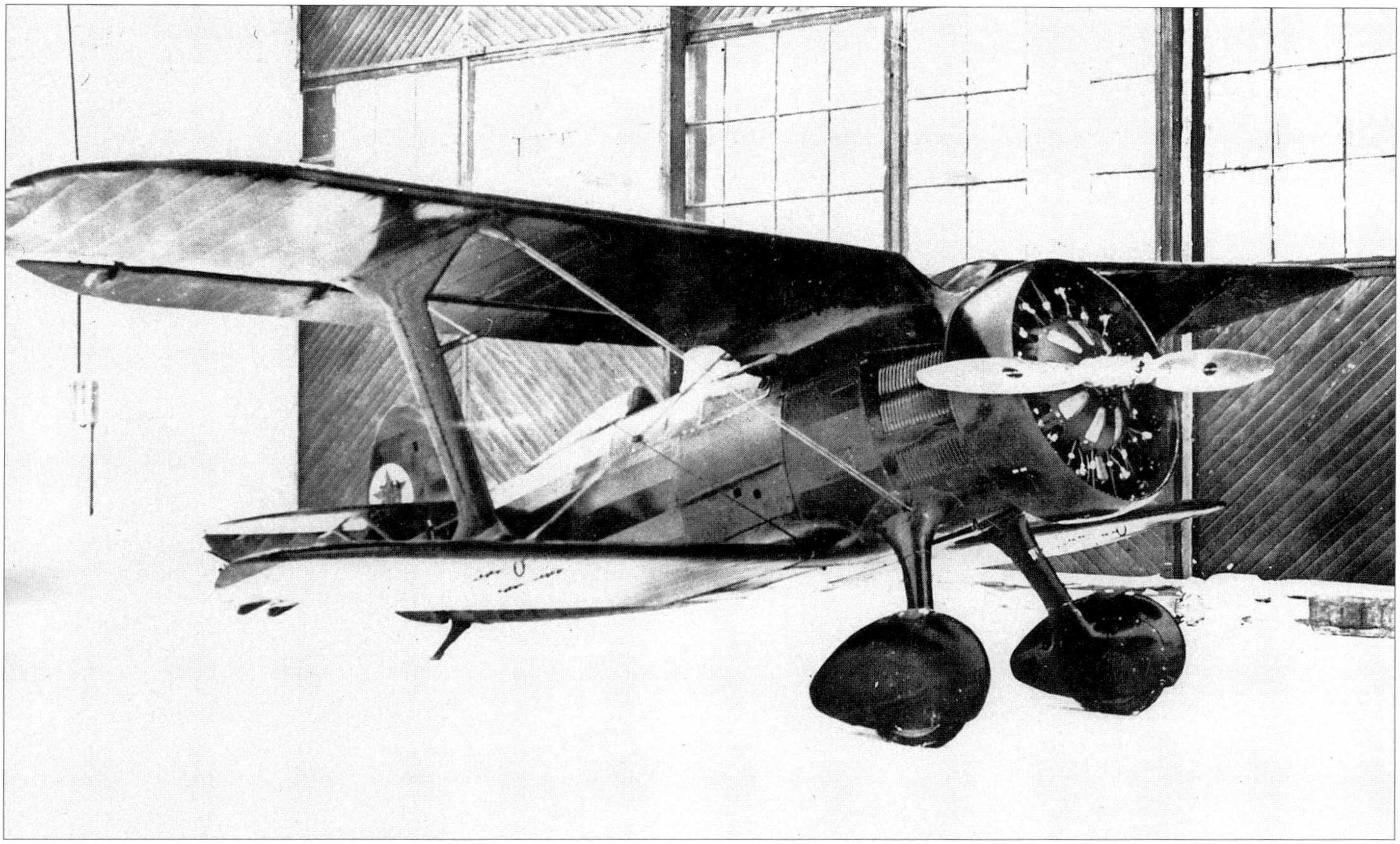

Above and below: As initially completed (December 1933) the second prototype TsKB-3 was identical to the first aircraft, except for the carefully faired and spatted wheeled undercarriage and the two unobtrusive aerial struts near the tips of the upper wings. Note the Hamilton Standard logo on the propeller blades.

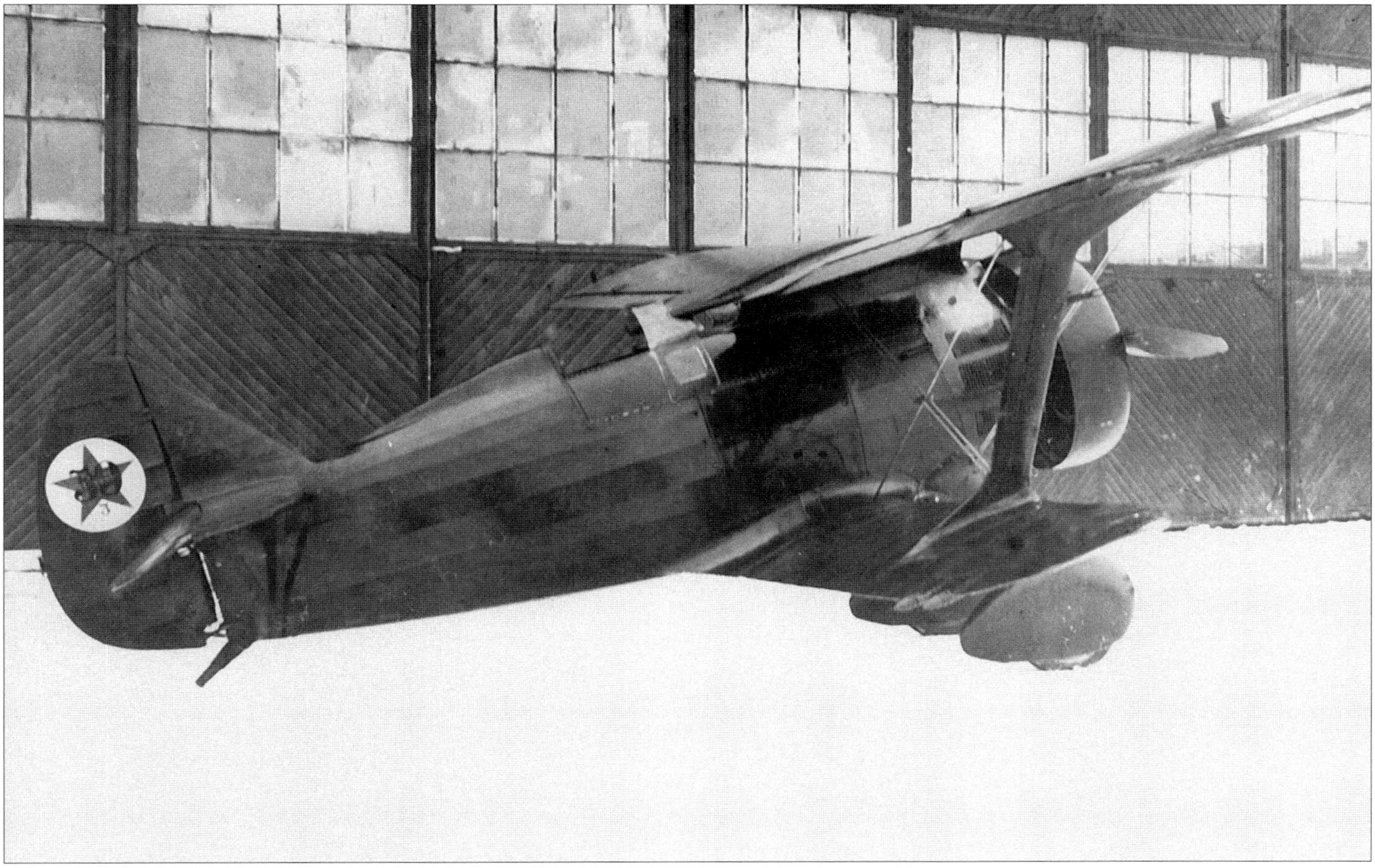

Above and below: Two more views of the first prototype on skis shortly before its landing accident on 23rd November 1933.

Above and below: The first production I-15 built by plant No. 39 (c/n 33903) at the factory airfield in 1934.

Above: The second prototype TsKB-3 at Kacha airfield in April 1934 during State Acceptance Trials, showing to advantage the redesigned Townend ring.

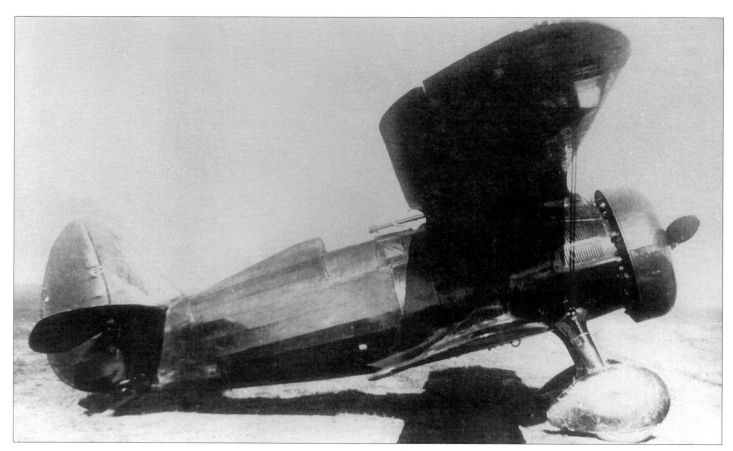

Another view of the modified second prototype at Kacha, showing the enlarged vertical tail.

Above: One of the first production I-15s built by aircraft factory No. 1.

'4 Red', a production I-15 fitted with RO-82 rocket launch rails for RS-82 unguided rockets, undergoing trials in 1937.

Another view of I-15 '4 Red' with six RS-82 rockets during trials.

turning turtle in a forced landing after a ski undercarriage bracing wire broke in flight. Happily the pilot was unhurt. One problem noted was directional instability at speeds exceeding 250 km/h (155 mph) but this was improved by fitting a larger vertical tail.

In December 1933 the second prototype was completed and used for the State Acceptance Trials which took barely a month. Initially this aircraft was almost identical to the first prototype, except for two small aerial struts near the tips of the upper wings. A spatted wheeled undercarriage was fitted this time in place of the skis. Pilots taking part in the trials were V. A. Stepanchonok, Tomas P. Suzi and A. I. Filin, all of whom lavished praise on the fighter's ease of handling, good control response and rate of climb.

Only two months later the Polikarpov TsKB-12 (I-16) monoplane fighter also started its State Acceptance Trials. This must have raised the self-esteem of the chief designer and his team and in September 1933 it was even further elevated when his Brigade was transformed into an OKB. Only a short while earlier many of the team had been in prison, and now they had two fighter designs about to go into service with the Soviet Air Force.

Before the evaluations were even finished preparations had started to mass-produce the TsKB-3, now redesignated I-15 for service in the VVS, at the two Moscow plants, No. 1 and No. 39. On 28th August 1934 the first series production aircraft from *zavod* 39, with construction number 33903 (ie, TsKB-3, plant

No. 39, third aircraft built) was flown and the following day the fighter went to NII VVS for its tests. These were completed on 11th September after only ten flights during which a maximum speed of 367 km/h (228 mph) was recorded.

The first series aircraft from *zavod* 1 (construction number 5648) entered flight test on 23rd November 1934 and once again poor weight control proved a problem. *Zavod* 1's aircraft was 30 kg (66 lb) heavier than I-15 c/n 33903. Performance, particularly at low level, was adversely affected, the maximum speed at sea level being reduced significantly. Other faults noted were an unsatisfactory finish, poor-quality undercarriage attachments and, most importantly, there was a tendency for the wing skin to rip off during flight.

Most of the initial production aircraft in 1934 had imported Wright SGR-1820-F3 Cyclone engines but the remainder received the M-25, a licence-built version of the Cyclone. It was intended that all of 1935 production should have the M-25, but some acquired the less powerful M-22 rated at 480 hp (358 kW), which degraded performance. Townend-ring cowlings were used, although one of the prototypes had a narrower-chord NACA type. In place of the prototypes' 3.0 m (9.8 ft) diameter wooden airscrew a metal 2.9 m (9.5 ft) diameter, statically adjustable propeller with three settings, was installed. Spinners were not fitted as standard.

The armament was four PV-1 machineguns, each with 750 rounds, and there was

provision for four 10-kg (22-lb) bombs or chemical weapon containers on D-1 carriers under each wing. At some stage armour was added to the pilot's seat.

Two more I-15 prototypes, both with Wright SGR-1820-F3 Cyclone engines, were flight-tested in 1937. One, with ski landing gear, was tested with six rocket projectiles mounted under the lower wings. Unfortunately the extra drag reduced the top speed at 2,400 m (7,900 ft) by 15 km/h (9 mph), the service ceiling decreased by 1,400 m (4,600 ft) and the climb to 5,000 m (16,400 ft) was increased by 2.6 minutes.

On the second aircraft a high-altitude pressure cabin (type SK-IV) designed by Aleksandr Ya. Schcherbakov was installed in 1938; see I-15V entry for more details

Production continued throughout 1935 but contradictory reports were emanating from the VVS. Many operational pilots were enthusiastic about the I-15 but the higher officials wanted production halted and refused to allow the production rate to increase to its maximum. Among the reasons given was the poor view from the cockpit during landing and take-off and a directional instability so great that it adversely affected accurate firing of the guns. This criticism was supported by a high accident rate in I-15 units. Polikarpov repeatedly tried to demonstrate that this criticism was unfair and that the solution was better training. He arranged for wind tunnel tests and demonstration flights but the latter were inconclusive due to the lack of inertia-free flight data recorders at that time. However, a special study conducted at TsAGI showed that with the gull-wing configuration directional stability improved as speed increased. It is clear that, rightly or wrongly, the gull-wing arrangement was not acceptable to the decision makers in the VVS and production of the I-15 stopped at the end of 1935, the last two reaching completion in 1936. So strong were the 'anti-Chaika' feelings that it was demanded that the type be withdrawn from VVS service; Polikarpov only managed to avoid this by a personal appeal to Stalin.

Early in 1936 Polikarpov was appointed Chief Designer of the OKBs at two factories: *zavod* No. 84 in Moscow and *zavod* No. 21 in Gor'kiy. The latter had, at that time, no prototype manufacturing facilities and it took the whole of 1936 to create them. Nonetheless the replacement for the I-15 was developed.

Structural description of the I-15

A single-bay sesquiplane of mixed construction, it was characterised by the gull-shaped formation of its upper wings. Welded KhMA steel tubes formed the main frame of the fuselage, which was similar in construction to that of the I-5, and rolled duralumin in an L-shaped section, added as a secondary structure, ensured a streamlined shape to the fuselage. Again light removable D1 duralumin panels covered the nose as far back as the cockpit and were attached to the supporting stringers and bulkheads. Doped linen fabric covered the rear fuselage, with double seam lacing and calico strips. The cockpit was fitted with a windscreen but was otherwise open and the pilot's seat was made of riveted dural sheets, allowing provision for a parachute as a cushion

Goettingen-436 aerofoil section was used for the wings which were of internally braced two-spar wooden construction with ribs; however, structural members were steel and there was a set of ten bracing wires. Steel tubes were integrated into the fuselage structure and inclined at 30° to form the 'gull' junction. Large Frise-type ailerons were used but only on the upper wings and had a fabric covered D6 alloy frame. The wings were fabric covered, apart from plywood leading edges extending to the front mainspar. A new feature was the use of streamlined I-shaped interwing struts made of KhMA steel tubes with light duralumin fairings.

A slightly smaller vertical tail than that of the I-5 was used on the prototype but was replaced by a much taller one on all subsequent airframes. The D6 duralumin structure was covered by a fabric skin and control hinges were accessed through spring-loaded flaps to ease maintenance. To support the horizontal tail, V-struts linked it with the fuselage.

Above: The starboard side of the fuselage with the fabric skin removed and the rearmost metal skin panel hinged upwards.

Above: The port side of the forward fuselage, showing the two portside PV-1 machine-guns and their ammunition boxes. The arrow with the '1' points to a bulged panel covering the engine crankcase/engine bearer joint.

The starboard side of the first prototype TsKB-3.

Above: The cockpit windshield, showing joint plates, the OP-1 optical gunsight and the backup KP-5 ring sight. Note that the reticle of the KP-1 has been folded back for safety reasons during ground handling.

Above: Close-up of the wheel spats. These were found to be prone to clogging with grass, the wheels jamming and the aircraft overturning as a result, and thus were usually removed in service.

The ski undercarriage of the first prototype with bracing wires. The skis were of the same type as used on the Grigorovich I-Z fighter.

Cantilever legs were used for the main undercarriage, with integral oleo shock absorbers having a 190-mm (7.5-in.) stroke. To prevent rotation of the piston inside the cylinder a torque link was provided. There was no axle connecting the two wheels and the wheel track was 1.6 m (4.9 ft), with braked wheels 700 x 100 mm (27.5 x 3.9 in.). The first prototype was fitted with 1,650 x 370 mm (65 x 14.5 in.) skis which were available for later aircraft when required. Wheel spats were fitted to the prototypes and to production aircraft but were often discarded in service. As on later models of the I-5, the tailskid moved synchronously with the rudder.

Prototypes and early production aircraft had imported Wright SGR-1820-F3 Cyclone engines which delivered 630 hp (470 kW) at sea level increasing to 715 hp (533 kW) at 2,000 m (6,500 ft). It was intended to replace these on the production lines by the licence-built M-25, but as its availability was delayed, the 480-hp (358-kW) M-22 was substituted for a short time. Archival records are ambiguous as to how many I-15s received the M-22 but at least 31 such aircraft were received in Spain by the Republican government.

While the prototypes had 3.0 m (9.8 ft) diameter Hamilton Standard propellers, series aircraft received 2.9 m (9.5 ft) diameter Soviet-produced two-blade fixed-pitch airscrews. Engines were cowled by a Townend ring but one test aircraft was given a narrower NACA type semi-cowling.

The armament was four synchronised 7.62 mm PV-1 machine-guns with an OP-1 telescopic sight surmounted with a KP-5 ring sight. Each gun had 750 rounds of ammunition. It was also possible to fit four DER-32 underwing bomb racks to carry up to 40 kg (88 lb) of bombs in 'overload condition'.

Production figures, which totalled 384 for Soviet-built I-15s, are shown below.

Number of aircraft built at:

	zavod 1 imeni Aviakhima	zavod 39 imeni Menzhinskovo
1934	60	34
1935	273	15
1936	2	
Total	**335**	**49**

Some archival records suggest that 276 I-15s were built in 1935 and none in 1936, thus making a total of 385 produced in the USSR. The destiny of this extra aircraft is a mystery but what is known is that it was not delivered to the usual military and civil authorities but went to some unspecified source.

Alfonso Barbeta, a director of CASA, recalled that another 287 I-15s were built under licence by the Republican side during the Spanish Civil War. This accords with the Nationalists' claim that 205 engineless airframes were found stored in the Reus factory and Republican records of approximately 80 Spanish-built I-15s being delivered to their squadrons from August 1937. Assembly of the aircraft took place at State Aircraft Factories No. 3 in Reus and No. 16 in Sabadell.

Spanish-built aircraft were intended to be identical to those produced in the Soviet Union with the 710-hp (530-kW) M-25 engine, but there were inevitably small differences such as a slightly different cowling and pilot's door and also the undercarriage lacked hooks for fastening the fairings. It was reported that some aircraft had flaps fitted to their lower wings. Whenever they were available ShKAS machine-guns ([*poolemyot*] *Shpitahl'novo i Komarnitskovo, aviatsionnyy, skorostrel'nyy* – Shpital'nyy and Komarnitskiy Fast Firing Aircraft Machine-Gun), with a rate of fire of 1,800 rounds per minute, were fitted in place of the PV-1 which could only manage 750 rounds per minute. The only components not manufactured locally were the Soviet-built engines and machine-guns.

In the Republican *Fuerzas Aéreas*, Spanish-built I-15s carried on the sides of their fuselage a black or white two- or three-digit serial prefixed CA (*Construcciones Aeronauticas*) or CC; Soviet-built examples carried only a white tail number.

I-15 aircraft were known in Spain by their nickname, *Chato*, Pugnose.

Operational history of the I-15

In Soviet service the operational life of the I-15 was surprisingly brief. Prejudice on the part of members of the VVS High Command against the gull wings caused the cessation of production at the end of 1935 after only 384 had been manufactured. Attempts were also made to withdraw the type from VVS service. Although this ploy failed it comes as no surprise to discover that it was supplied in significant numbers from VVS stock to the Spanish Republicans and also probably to the Mongolian Air Force.

Those aircraft sent to Spain were in answer to a call for assistance from the Republican Popular Front Government, which was a coalition of socialist and communist parties. On 18th July 1936 the fascist so-called 'Nationalist' rebellion against the Republican government of Spain was initiated. Italy and Germany supplied help and arms to the Nationalists and at the end of August 1936 I. V. Stalin agreed to the first delivery of aircraft to the Republicans. On 13th October 1936 the Soviet cargo ship S/S *Staryy Bol'shevik* (Old Bol'shevik; a phrase meaning 'a long-time Bol'shevik uncompromisingly true to the cause of the Party')

Test pilot Edgard Preman beside an I-15; note the uncowled engine on this aircraft.

unloaded crates containing 18 M-22 engine I-15 fighters at Cartagena. They were transported to Los Alcazares where Soviet engineers quickly assembled them, together with another seven that arrived on the S/S *Lava Mendi* three days later. A further six docked on 23rd October in the S/S *Gheorgi Dimitrov*.

Two squadrons (*escuadrillas*), each of 12 aircraft, were formed plus an attrition reserve. Flown at that time by mainly Soviet volunteers, the squadrons were named after their commanders 'Pablo Palancar' (the *nom de guerre* of Major Pavel Rychagov) and 'Antonio' (Major Sergei Tarkhov) and were soon put into action in the first battle for Madrid. The 'Palancar' squadron was based at El Soto 26 km (16 miles) north-east of the capital and

'Antonio' at Alcalá de Henares 29 km (19 miles) east. A number of Spanish pilots arrived to serve with the squadrons in November and affectionately named the I-15 'Chato'. By March 1937 the *Chato* pilots numbered six Americans, one Guatemalan and several Frenchmen. More Spaniards were training in the Soviet Union but these did not complete their course until July 1937 when large numbers started returning to the fight.

Later a 'Basque' squadron was formed when 15 *Chatos*, also with M-22 engines, were unloaded at Bilbao on 15th November from the 'Andrei'. Commanded by 'Boris' (Major Maranchov), they were based at La Albericia. On 2nd January 1937 a second batch of 15 or 16 *Chatos* was unloaded at Santander.

Basic specifications of the I-15

	Second prototype TsKB-3 with Hamilton propeller	I-15 *zavod* 1 series production with fixed-pitch propeller
Span:		
upper wings	9.75 m (32.0 ft)	9.75 m (32.0 ft)
lower wings	7.5 m (24.6 ft)	7.5 m (24.6 ft)
Length	6.1 m (20.0 ft)	6.1 m (20.0 ft)
Wing area	23.55 m² (253 sq. ft)	23.55 m² (253 sq. ft)
Weight:		
empty	949 kg (2,093 lb)	983 kg (2,168 lb)
loaded	1,358 kg (2,994 lb)	1,389 kg (3,063 lb)
Maximum speed:		
at sea level	324 km/h (201 mph)	315 (198 mph)
at 3,000 m (9,840 ft)	353 km/h (219 mph)	367 (228 mph)
Climb to 5,000 m (16,400 ft)	6.0 minutes	6.2 minutes
Service ceiling	8,000 m (26,250 ft)	9,800 m (32,150 ft)
Time to complete 360° turn	8 seconds	9 seconds
Take-off run	n.a.	70 m (230 ft)
Landing run	n.a.	70 m (230 ft)
Landing speed	85 km/h (53 mph)	90 km/h (56 mph)

I. U. Pavlov beside his I-15 wearing the same colour scheme as the I-5 he had flown earlier, complete with *Za VKP(b)* dedication. Note the 'hammered effect' polish on the metal skin panels.

The first success of the *Chatos* was achieved on 4th November 1936 when a Junkers Ju 52/3m of *Kampfstaffel* Moreau and two Fiat C.R.32s were shot down by I-15s over Humanes; a second Ju 52/3m was so badly damaged that it made a forced landing at Esquivas. On the same day eleven I-15s led by 'Palancar' attacked nine Heinkel He 51s near Madrid and shot down four of them. None of the *Chatos* was seriously damaged in either engagement, although two landed behind Nationalist lines and were captured after running out of fuel.

An even greater achievement was recorded when half of the 'Palancar' squadron deployed to Aragon in late November. Under the leadership of Ivan Kopets it destroyed the first all-Spanish *escuadrilla* of the Nationalists which consisted of six Heinkel He 51s. One was shot down, four destroyed later when caught unawares on Caude airfield, and the sixth was written off in an accident.

Led by 'Casimiro' (Anton Kovalevskiy), the other half of the squadron had moved to Tabernas, near Málaga, in an attempt to stem the Nationalist drive up the coast.

For the rest of 1936 the other *Chatos* defended Madrid with such success that the Nationalists abandoned daytime bombing of the city and resorted to night attacks. Historians largely attribute the failure of the Nationalists to capture the capital in this offensive to the boost given to the morale of the defenders by the arrival and effectiveness of the Soviet fighters. A heavy price was paid by the two *Chato* squadrons; nine aircraft were lost in battle and, tragically, Major Tarkhov was killed by Madrileños who mistook him for a German after he parachuted from his stricken aircraft.

Squadron commanders were frequently changed. In addition to the replacement of Tarkhov by 'Kozakov' (Major Aleksandr Osadchiy), 'Palancar' was supplanted in December by 'José' (Major Ivan Kopets) who, when promoted in January 1937, was succeeded by Andrés García Lacalle.

On 8th March 1937 the Battle of Guadalajara began and an Italian motorised column attempting to encircle Madrid from the northeast was constantly attacked by Republican aircraft, of which a significant number were *Chatos*. The encirclement was averted and the Republican army gained a decisive victory, turning the retreat of the Italians into a rout.

After the Nationalists failed to capture Madrid they turned their attention to eliminating the Basque enclave in the north and began their offensive on 31st March 1937. In May, 15 *Chatos* of the 'Lacalle' squadron with Spanish pilots made several attempts to reinforce their beleaguered colleagues but, through a combination of bad weather and worse luck, only eight managed to reach their goal.

A delivery of 31 M-25 or Cyclone-engined *Chatos* to Cartagena on the S/S *Aldecoa* on 14th February enabled the Republicans, in spite of large losses, to rebuild their stock to 30 machines by the end of March 1937. This number of airworthy aircraft was more or less maintained until the end of the year when it started to fall as a consequence of attrition

3 Red, a standard Soviet Air Force I-15, is prepared for a sortie. Note that the aircraft still has wheel spats.

from intensive ground attack operations and a shortage of spares.

Deliveries of I-15s from the USSR continued until the end of July 1937, by which time two more consignments of 31 had docked. At least one, but probably both consignments, was of *Chatos* with Cyclone or M-25 engines. Aircraft were despatched from the Soviet Union in batches of 31 which was the size of a VVS fighter squadron (*eskadril'ya*); the regimental (*polk*) system was not introduced into the VVS until April 1939. There is some dispute among aircraft historians as to the number of I-15 fighters that arrived in Spain. One holds that there were five complete batches, each of 31, making a total of 155, another that one of the batches was incomplete and only 153 actually arrived, and yet a third maintains that the number was as low as 139. It is doubtful whether these discrepancies will ever be resolved because full records of the deliveries have never been found. For the purpose of this book it is assumed that 155 is the correct number.

The arrival of more aircraft enabled a small detachment with William Labussière in charge to be formed at Carmoli for coastal patrol work in February 1937 but this was

Right: When the Spanish Civil War erupted in 1936, pilots from many nations joined the International Brigades to assist the Republicans. Here, two of the volunteers, one of them in leather flying breeches, pose beside a *Fuerzas Aéreas* I-15. This view shows the forward fuselage details and the engine's individual exhaust stubs.

Below: An early-production I-15 with wheel spats. Note the drop tank attachment fittings under the lower wings.

Above: A Spanish Republican I-15, apparently with no identification stripes on the wings. The I-15 was called 'Curtiss' or 'Boeing' by the Nationalists who mistakenly believed it to be a version of either the Curtiss F9C Sparrowhawk or the Boeing F4B-4.

'19 White', a Republican I-15, showing to advantage the red identification stripes under both upper and lower wings.

Above: A Spanish Republican pilot poses in the cockpit of I-15 CA-232. This aircraft was captured by the Nationalists in 1939.

Republican pilots walk away from the flight line after a mission as the ground crews get busy with one of the squadron's *Chatos*.

Above: Still in Republican colours, this *Chato* is seen after capture by the Nationalists at La Rabaza airfield.

I-15 CA-142 of the 1st *Escuadrilla de Chatos*, showing the unit's Mickey Mouse emblem on the tail.

Above: A Spanish-built I-15 during a test flight, with national insignia and serial still to be applied.

This I-15 was operated by the 2nd *Escuadrilla de Chatos*, as indicated by the penguin emblem on the fuselage. The location of the squadron emblem varied from aircraft to aircraft.

Above and below: This Soviet-built I-15 (as indicated by the serial '19 White' lacking the CA prefix) was the first example captured by the Nationalists. It is seen at Carreno in October 1937. Note the Fiat C.R.32s lined up in the background in the lower photo, including at least one flown by the *Patrulla Azúl* (Blue Patrol).

Two views of I-15 '3-164' in company with a Heinkel He 70F-2, a Junkers Ju 52/3m and a Savoia Marchetti S.M.79. Interestingly, the aircraft still has early-style black Nationalist roundels on the fuselage (though the arrows appear to have been painted out) but carries the new-style red/yellow roundels on the wings.

Romulo Negrin poses beside his *Chato* (CC-011). The CC prefix to the serial is noteworthy, as it was more commonly used for Republican I-15*bis Super Chatos*.

reabsorbed into the 'Lacalle' squadron in May. In addition, a fourth *Chato* squadron was created for the Aragon front in April 1937 and based at Algete. It was commanded by Roberto Alfonso Santamaria.

A reorganisation took place in May and the squadrons were reformed and also numbered: the 1st *Escuadrilla de Chatos* commanded by 'Ramón' (Major Yeriomenko) at Teruel; the 2nd *Escuadrilla de Chatos* was led by Roberto Alfonso Santamaria and based at Castejon del Puente; and a 3rd *Escuadrilla de Chatos*, with 'Kozakov' (Aleksandr Osadchiy) in charge, was located at Campo Soto. At La Albericia the isolated Basque squadron, commanded by Manuel Aguirre, remained unnumbered.

At first the Republican *Chato* squadrons had been part of *Grupo de Caza* (Group) No.

12 commanded by Arkadiy Zlatotsvetov. In this unit they were grouped together with all the other Soviet squadrons flying the I-16, Polikarpov R-5 reconnaissance aircraft and Tupolev SB 2M-100 bomber. By December 1936 sufficient numbers of aircraft were available for the I-15 and I-16 fighter squadrons to be formed into a separate Group which was given the number 21. Three months later Group 26 was created for sole control of the *Chato* squadrons. Ivan Kopets was placed in charge of this Group where he remained until April when he was replaced by Yevgeniy Ptookhin. From mid-October Group 26 was put under Spanish control with Juan José Armario as the first officer in charge, 'General Douglas' (Brigade Commander Yakov V. Smooshkevich) was in overall command of all Soviet aviation forces in Spain.

In July 1937 Anatoliy Serov, a flight commander of the 1st *Escuadrilla*, was provisionally given permission to form a *Patrulla de Noche* (night fighter flight) with six I-15s and success followed when a Junkers Ju 52/3m was shot down on 26th July. Although the unit remained in existence till February 1939, the scarce resources available were being underused and therefore additional daytime ground attacks were introduced. *Chatos* used as night fighters had ring manifolds redirecting the engine's exhaust under the fuselage to avoid impairing the pilot's night vision.

Modest supplies of Spanish-built I-15s began to reach the squadrons in August 1937 and in September the 4th *Escuadrilla de Chatos* under Ladislao Duarte Espes was formed at Sabadell, Barcelona. In March 1938 José Falco Sanmartín attempted to form a 5th *Escuadrilla de Chatos* at Sabadell but after a few days it was disbanded when it was realised there were not enough aircraft to justify another squadron and still maintain an adequate attrition reserve.

Battles continued to rage in the south and the *Chatos* were prominent in the Battle of Brunete, just to the south-east of Madrid. On one occasion two squadrons together with three squadrons of I-16 *Moscas*, about 50 fighters in total, fought a pitched battle with 60 Fiat C.R.32s and 12 Heinkel He 51s. For the loss of two *Moscas* and three *Chatos*, eight C.R.32s and one He 51 were shot down.

By September 1937 the *Chatos* were operating mainly in Aragon and Catalonia and this situation continued until the end of the war. One spectacular success was achieved on 15th October when 15 *Chatos* escorted by 43 *Moscas* made a dawn raid on Garrapinillos airfield near Zaragoza, claiming the destruction of 26 Nationalist aircraft, including two Messerschmitt Bf 109s that attempted to take off to intercept them.

When the Nationalists finally overran the northern enclave at the end of October 1937 the remnants of the 2nd *Escuadrilla*, unable to rejoin their comrades in the south, flew to neutral France.

Mid-December 1937 saw the opening of the Republican attack on Teruel, with heavy participation by the four *Chato* squadrons. Losses were higher than replacements and by mid-March 1938 there were only 15 flyable I-15s left. Although no more *Chatos* arrived from the USSR, the Spanish factories at Reus and Sabadell were supplying increasing numbers of repaired and newly-built I-15s and the number of serviceable *Chatos* gradually built up to a maximum of 70 by October 1938. However, this number was sustainable for only a short period and losses once again mounted as an increasing number of ground attacks were made in desperate attempts to stop the advancing Nationalists. Republican

An I-15 (CA-155?) operated by a *Patrulla de Noche* is refuelled for a night sortie.

airfields and aircraft plants were captured, thereby inhibiting repairs, and by the end of March 1939 the stock of operable aircraft was exhausted.

On 1st February 1939 the Nationalists had captured 18 I-15s on Vich airfield. Of these, six were airworthy, and by taking those into operation in addition to others that had been repaired after capture, a squadron of *Chatos* was formed. Designated at that time *Grupo* 1-G-8, the new unit was formed from 1-G-2 whose pilots had been flying Heinkel He 51 fighters. In Nationalist service the *Chato* was known as Type 8. No evidence has been found to indicate that there was any confrontation between *Chatos* of the Republicans and those of the Nationalists.

Slow-flying bombers, such as the Junkers Ju 52/3m, had been easy targets for the *Chato* pilots and the Heinkel He 51 fighters, which were slower, less manoeuvrable and more lightly armed than the I-15, were also comfortably outclassed. Until the arrival of the Nationalist monoplane fighters the only type whose capabilities matched the I-15 was the Fiat C.R.32. The Italian machine was slightly faster on the level but lost out on rate of climb and manoeuvrability; still, its superior diving speed could often be relied upon to save its skin when confronted with the *Chato*'s four 7.62-mm machine-guns which were more effective than the Fiat's twin 12.7-mm guns, particularly in close combat. The advent of the Messerschmitt Bf 109 and Fiat G 50 monoplanes showed up the inadequacies of the I-15 but the monoplanes could be caught out if they ventured too close or their pilots became over-confident. Furthermore, when bombers such as the Heinkel He 111 arrived, they proved to be faster than the *Chatos*, which then came to be used more frequently in the ground attack role.

Chatos proved very popular with their pilots, not only on account of their excellent manoeuvrability, but also for their stout structure with its ability to absorb a great deal of punishment. Aircraft had been known to return to base with as many as 80 hits; an added bonus was its reluctance to catch fire, unlike its compatriot, the Tupolev SB bomber. Another invaluable asset of the *Chato* was its ability to take off and land in a very short distance enabling it to use improvised and bomb-damaged airfields from which such types as the I-16 could not operate. Ground crews also appreciated the relative ease with which it could be patched up and repaired; fuselage panels could be easily removed and the air-cooled radials were simpler to maintain than liquid-cooled in-line engines. One serious design fault was discovered in tragic circumstances. The bomb release lever was too close to the control lever for the engine cooling vents and when José Cuatero was taking off for a bombing mission he inadvertently pulled the wrong lever and in the resulting explosion killed himself and the pilot of the aircraft in front of him. Both *Chatos* were destroyed and a third was damaged.

Misconceptions arose from the Western observers' habit of referring to the I-15 as a 'Curtiss' simply because it bore a resemblance to biplane fighters manufactured by that American company. Journalists and experts, who should have known better, too readily assumed that it must be a copy of a Western type. The same mistake was made with reference to Japanese aircraft and we later paid a terrible price in blood for such arrogance.

Several I-15s which had been flown to France and French North Africa at the end of the war were returned to the new government. Others had been surrendered to avoid reprisals or were captured and many were found incomplete at the Reus factory. After the war the Nationalists placed all airworthy *Chatos* totalling 44 aircraft into *Escuadra num* 32 which was based first at Manises near Valencia but later moved to La Rabasa (Alicante). The *Escuadra* was redesignated *Regimiento de Asalto num* 32 in 1940. After the war incomplete *Chato* airframes found at the factory by the Nationalists were made airworthy and formed into Regimiento 33 at Villanubla near Valladolid. By March 1940 the *Ejercito del Aire* had 53 flyable *Chatos* and another 72 retained in storage to be cannibalised for spare parts. The type code was changed to A4 in 1945 and the *Chatos* remained in service until the beginning of the 1950s. It must be said that their long service was probably more attributable to the Allied embargo on supplies of military equipment to fascist Spain rather than to the excellence of the design.

I-15 survivors

There are no examples of the I-15 extant but a replica is on show in the *Museo del Aire*, near Madrid; one side is painted in Republican and the other in Nationalist colours.

I-15 world altitude record breaker

No official designation is known for the lightened I-15 specially modified for an attempt on the world altitude record set in April 1934 by R. Donatti flying a Caproni Ca 114A. The aircraft was, in fact, the original first prototype TsKB-3 which, as already recounted, had

The TsKB-3 No. 1 following extensive modifications for an attempt on the world altitude record. Note the translucent wing skin, the modified landing gear struts lacking shock absorbers and the barograph mounted on the starboard upper wing to record the altitude.

This page:

Top: The I-15V (*ob''yekt* 415V) was an extensively modified I-15 featuring a pressure cabin designed in-house and an M-25E engine with twin superchargers. The cockpit canopy of this aircraft offered the pilot a much better view than the competing pressure cabin designs originating from the Schcherbakov OKB!

Centre: Three-quarters rear view of the I-15V (*ob''yekt* 415V) from starboard, showing the NACA cowling and the three-bladed propeller. The large chin fairing housed an intercooler to which compressed air from both superchargers was fed.

Bottom: Close-up of the cowling, showing the starboard TK-1 supercharger.

Opposite page:

Top left: The port side of the I-15V (*ob''yekt* 415V) with the canopy open. The greater part of the metal skin panels has been removed, showing that the pressure cabin is a fairly large 'cocoon' inserted into the fuselage structure. Interestingly, the 'cocoon' features its own instrument panel, while the aircraft's original instrument panel can be seen further ahead! Apart from the traditional Soviet catch word Sekretno (secret), the photograph carries two dates: 25th October 1938 and 19th January 1939.

Top right: A starboard view of the 'unbuttoned' I-15V (*ob''yekt* 415V), showing the shape of the pressure cabin and the canopy hinged open to starboard.

Bottom left: The interior of the pressure cabin on the I-15V (*ob''yekt* 415V). The cockpit was extremely cramped and, considering the thick fur-lined clothing which was a must for high-altitude flying in those days, it obviously took a pilot of light build to fly the aircraft!

Bottom right: A full-scale mock-up of the Polikarpov pressure cabin. The mock-up differed considerably from the real thing, featuring a one-piece canopy with no fixed windshield. Interestingly, the optical gunsight was integrated into the canopy, swinging away together with it!

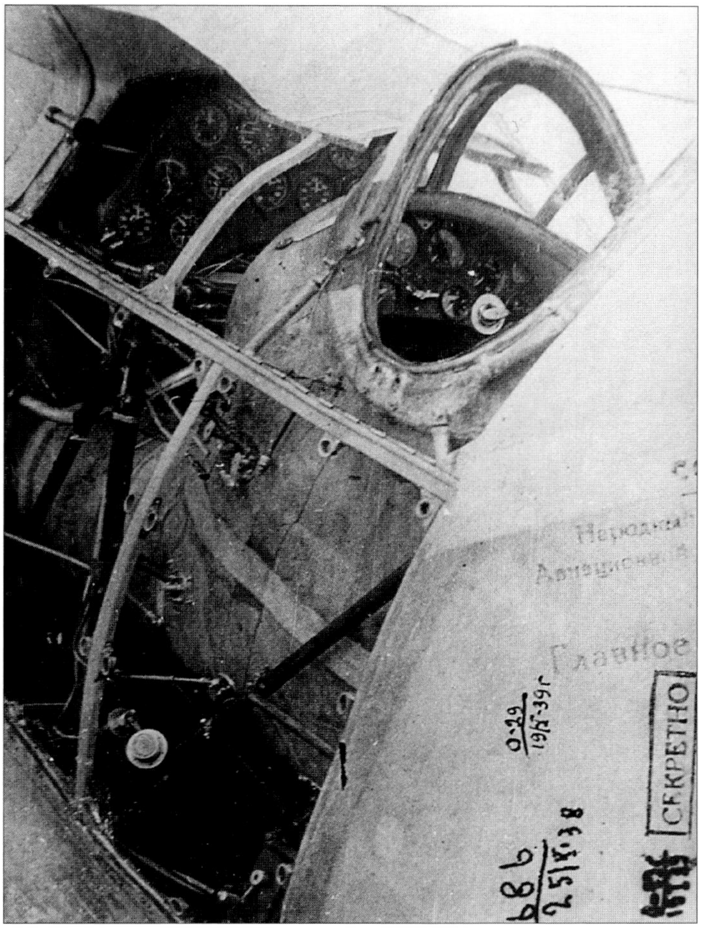
Главное
СЕКРЕТНО

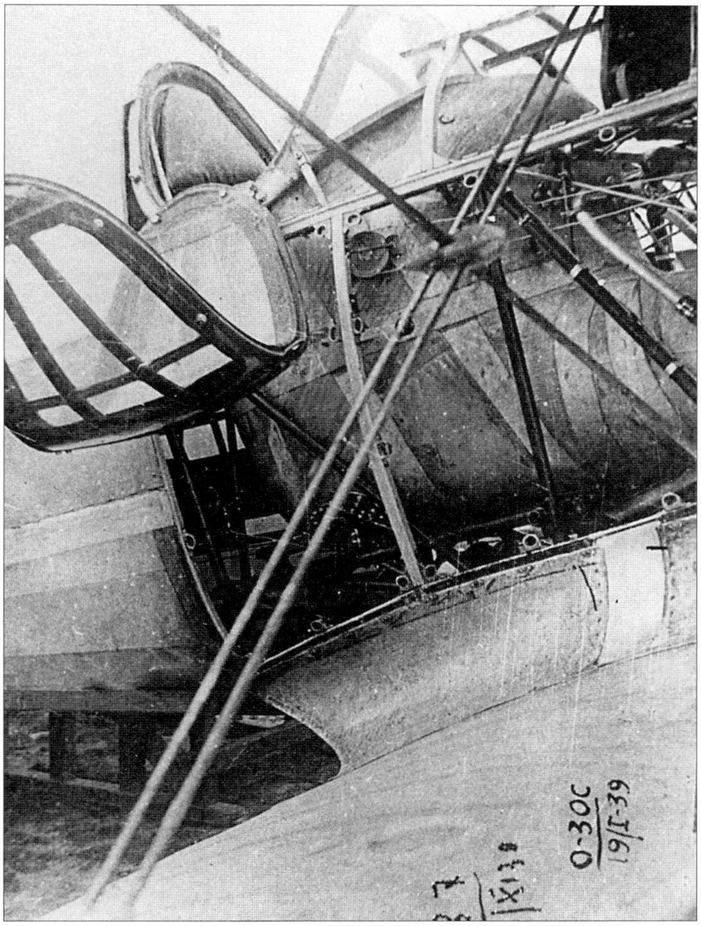

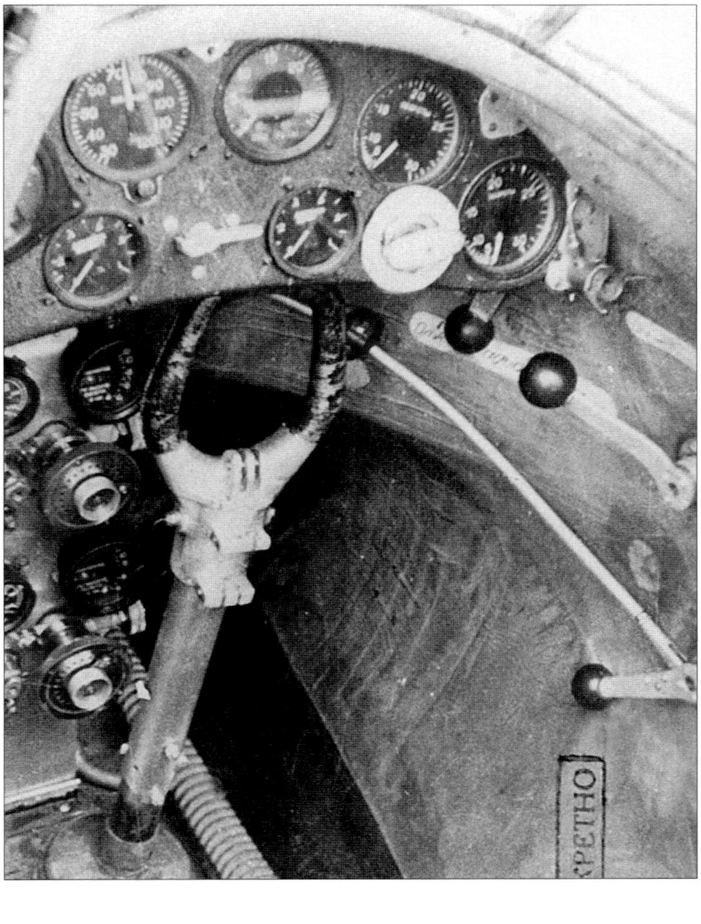

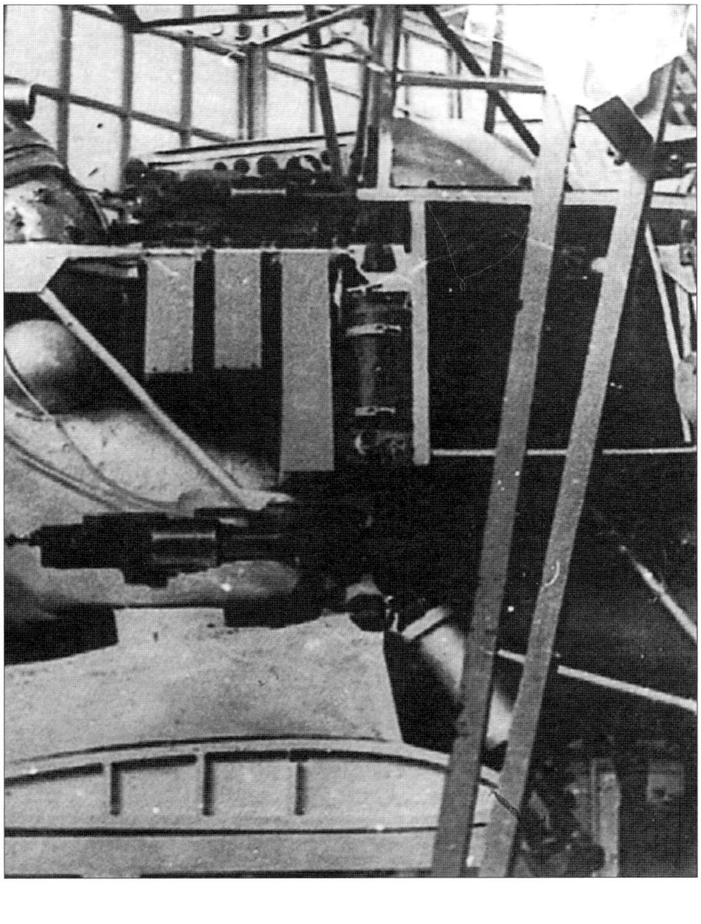

Above: The designation I-15V was also worn by a different high-altitude version with a pressure cabin developed by Aleksandr Ya. Schcherbakov. Here, this aircraft is shown at NII VVS during State Acceptance Trials (note the hexagonal concrete slabs of Schcholkovo airfield).

The same aircraft pictured a while earlier during manufacturer's flight tests. The curious-looking canopy with its many small 'portholes' is open; note the 'proboscis' at the front for the gunsight. The legend on the fuselage reads *Dayosh vysotu i skorost'* (Press on for [higher] speed and altitude!).

Above: A hitherto unpublished close-up of the cockpit canopy on Schcherbakov's version of the I-15V. The usefulness of the extensive glazing aft of the cockpit is questionable, since the pilot obviously couldn't see much through this 'sieve' over his head!

The inside of the hemispherical pressure portion of the canopy on Schcherbakov's I-15V. There are at least 18 separate windows in it!

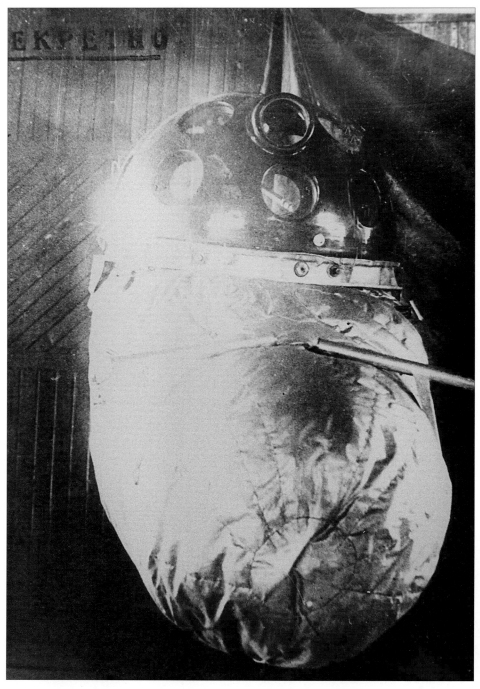

An overall view of Schcherbakov's pressure cabin. The thing looked like the monstrous many-eyed larva of some Martian insect.

been damaged in a crash landing on 23rd November 1933.

The aircraft was fitted with a Wright R-1820-F54 Cyclone engine having better high-altitude performance. All paint was stripped and the aft fuselage, wings and tail unit reskinned with a special thin fabric, making a substantial part of the airframe appear semi-translucent. Some instruments, the armament, the landing gear shock absorbers and the Townend ring were removed and even the pilot's seat replaced with a leather sling in order to save another few extra kilograms. Just enough fuel was filled for the

ascent, as the aircraft was to glide back to earth with the engine inoperative.

These drastic measures obviously paid off because on 21st November 1935, with Vladimir K. Kokkinaki at the controls, the aircraft reached an altitude of 14,575 m (47,821 ft), unofficially breaking Donatti's record by 142 m (465 ft). 'Official' status was denied to the accomplishment because the USSR was not, at that time, a member of the FAI.

I-15V (ob"yekt 415V)

Interest had been aroused by the success of Kokkinaki's attempt to beat the world altitude

record and on 30th December 1935 Polikarpov proposed a more radical solution for reaching an even higher altitude of 15,400 m (50,500 ft). Among the modifications made to the I-15 in pursuance of this goal was an increase of wing span to 12.0 m (39.4 ft) on the upper wings and 9.5 m (32.2 ft) on the lower plus a fully enclosed pressure cabin for the pilot. The proposal was accepted by GUAP and the second prototype TsKB-3, with an M-25E engine with two TK turbo-superchargers, was fitted with a pressure cabin developed by Polikarpov's OKB in 1937. A metal-reinforced canopy was hinged on the starboard side and given a rubber seal to achieve an air-tight joint. The aircraft was known as the I-15V (vysotnyy – high-altitude) or ob"yekt (object) 415V.

Development took a considerable time and on 26th January 1939 a special commission examined the aircraft. The commission was not impressed and thought it looked worn, recommending that this project be stopped and future work of this type be given to Schcherbakov's team at KB-5 in zavod 1.

I-15V

A high-altitude pressure cabin designed by A. Ya. Schcherbakov (type SK-IV) was installed on a prototype aircraft in 1938; confusingly, this aircraft was likewise designated I-15V. The cabin weighed 45.6 kg (100 lb), had rubber seals and circular windows in a metal windscreen. It scored over Polikarpov's design by ensuring that the pilot was comfortable without having to wear heavy winter flying clothes. Test pilots Stepan P. Sooproon and P. Ye. Loginov reported favourably on the aircraft, which successfully completed its factory and state tests. The maximum height reached was 9,450 m (31,000 ft), the limiting factor being the age of the aircraft's engine. It was decided not to replace it and development of the pressure cabin was transferred to more modern aircraft (see I-152GK, I-153V and I-153TKGK).

I-15M floatplane project

This was a 1937 project for a seaplane version (hence the M for morskoy, naval) intended to be catapult-launched from warships. It had one large underfuselage float flanked by two smaller underwing floats.

TsKB-42 Project

TsKB-42 was the designation of another projected, but never built, height record breaker. Plans included modifying the I-15 by installing a completely faired-in, high-altitude supercharged Wright Cyclone F-54 engine, adding a cockpit canopy, extending the upper wings by 5 m (7.4 ft) and the lower by 2.0 m (6.6 ft). No reasons were ever disclosed for its premature termination.

Chapter 4

I-15bis: Super-Chato

or Prejudice Prevails

I-15bis single-seat fighter (tip 32)

In 1935 *zavod* 39 manufactured a prototype which, in order to satisfy the VVS, was based on the I-15 but dispensed with the unpopular gull wings. No official designation has been found for this aircraft, but it was known under the factory name **TsKB-3 No. 7** (derived from the c/n, 339007). Additionally, its structure was reinforced, four PV-1 machine-guns fitted, various new pieces of equipment added and it was powered by a 715-hp (533-kW) Wright SGR-1820-F3 Cyclone engine. When it was tested by Edgard Preman at NII VVS between 21st May and 29th July 1935 it was found that the increase of 109 kg (240 lb) over the empty weight of the second prototype TsKB-3 had a deleterious effect on manoeuvrability, increasing the time taken to complete a 360° circle to 10 seconds. Likewise, the rate of climb fell from 15 m/sec (2,950 ft/min) to 12 m/sec (2,360 ft/min). Such a performance was not acceptable and a complete redesign of the aircraft into what ultimately became the **I-15bis** was agreed.

TsKB-3bis was the OKB designation of this new fighter; both designations indicated a second version of the I-15/TsKB-3. Apart from eliminating the gull-wing layout of the I-15, many additional changes were made, the most important of which was the overall strengthening of the structure to meet new requirements laid down in 1934. The recently developed 750-hp (560-kW) M-25V with a much wider NACA cowling and a metal fixed-pitch propeller with spinner was installed. Wheel spats were fitted as standard, although many were later removed. The four-gun armament was retained but some aircraft were given the alternative fit of two 12.5-mm (.49 calibre) BS machine-guns ([*poolemyot*] *Berezina sinkhronnyy*, Berezin's synchronised machine-gun).

State Acceptance Trials at NII VVS took place from 2nd to 29th July 1937; such was the haste that the not fully finished prototype was used, with disappointing results. Maximum speed remained the same as that of the

I-15 with a Wright SGR-1820-F3 Cyclone engine but rate of climb, and manoeuvrability in particular, had deteriorated. When comparing empty weights the I-15bis was nearly 300 kg (661 lb) heavier than the second prototype TsKB-3, and without increasing power a diminished performance was a foregone conclusion. A new propeller was then fitted but this failed to improve the situation. With regret the State Commission reported that the I-15bis had failed its State Acceptance Trials. However, pressure from the VVS High Command gained approval for series production to start, provided development continued.

Production started at *zavod* 1 in mid-1937 under the in-house code *tip* (type) 32 but bulk deliveries did not begin in earnest until 1938 and it is probable that some of the first batches were held back pending modifications. Progressive improvements continued to be made to the I-15bis after production had started: for example, the fuel capacity was increased from 260 to 310 litres (57 to 68 gal.)

The so-called TsKB-3 No.7 (c/n 339007) which was the immediate precursor of the I-15bis, still powered by a Wright Cyclone engine with a Townend ring but featuring a traditional wing box. The anti-gull wing lobby had won for the time being.

Above: The TsKB-3 No. 7 at the factory airfield of plant No. 39 in March 1935 during manufacturer's flight tests, with Tupolev TB-3 bombers in the background.
Below: This view shows clearly the new upper wing centre section.

Above and below: The same aircraft at the NII VVS airfield in Schcholkovo (now Chkalovskaya AB) near Moscow during State Acceptance Trials. Note that the fighter has been retrofitted with wheel spats at this stage to maximise speed.

Above and left: Two more views of the TsKB-3 No. 7 development aircraft at NII VVS. The VVS red star insignia are barely discernible under the lower wings. Note the exhaust collector in the photo on the left.

Below left: This looks like a drop tank but is in fact a gun pod with a 7.62-mm ShKAS machine-gun (note the barrel protruding from the lower forward section of the pod). Also of note is the ski landing gear.

and provision made for carrying two 80-litre (17.5-gal.) drop tanks under the lower wings.

It had been the intention of the VVS to replace the I-15*bis* on the production lines of *zavod* 1 in 1938 with a developed version designated I-152 (see separate entry) but this idea was abandoned, presumably the result of a decision taken on 23rd October 1937 to put the gull-winged I-153 biplane into production in 1939. The I-153 was to be powered by the new 800-hp (597-kW) M-62 engine and 25 (some sources suggest 27) I-15*bis* fighters were also built with this engine in 1939. One example (construction number 5237) was used for testing a new lubrication system.

Structural description of the I-15*bis*

Developed from the I-15, the I-15*bis* was a single-bay sesquiplane with classic biplane upper wings, but it was much more than just a rejection of the gull-wing configuration. A licence-built 750-hp (559-kW) M-25V high-altitude rated derivative of the Wright SGR-1820-F3 Cyclone was installed to drive a fixed-pitch two-blade metal propeller of 2.8 m (9.2 ft) diameter with a large spinner. A wider NACA type duralumin cowling was given adjustable louvres to control the airflow at different temperatures and two new exhaust gas ring manifolds were designed, of which one discharged on the starboard side and the other,

Above: The real prototype of the I-15*bis* differed from the TsKB-3 No. 7 development aircraft mainly in having an M-25V engine with a NACA cowling.

Right and below: Unlike the TsKB-3 No. 7 which wore standard green camouflage, the I-15*bis* prototype was attractively finished in silver dope with red trim. Note the small rear-vision windows in the headrest fairing (which were omitted on production examples) and the twin wire aerials stretched from the upper wings to the fin.

less obtrusively, lower down on the port side. The cowling fore section had three panels, one upper and two at the sides, and the aft section five panels, one upper, two side and two lower. Steel strips joined the panels which were attached to the fuselage frame by brackets. On top of the cowling was an intake duct for the oil cooler and carburettor. The fuel capacity was increased from 260 to 310 litres. In 1939 25 (or 27, sources differ) I-15*bis* were built with 800-hp (597-kW) M-62 engines.

Similar in construction to that of the I-15, the fuselage of the I-15*bis* had a main frame comprised of welded KhMA steel tubes with rolled duralumin L-shaped sections added as a secondary structure ensuring a streamlined shape to the fuselage. Once again, light removable D1 duralumin panels covered the nose as far back as the cockpit and were attached to the supporting stringers and bulkheads. Doped linen fabric covered the rear fuselage with double seam lacing and calico strips. The open cockpit was fitted with a windscreen and the pilot's seat was made of riveted duralumin sheets, allowing provision for a parachute as a cushion. Protection for the pilot was added in the form of a 9 mm (0.35 in.) thick armoured back to his seat.

The span of the upper wings was increased by 45 cm (17.7 in.) and a Clark 'YH' aerofoil section employed, but chord and thickness remained unchanged. The cabane struts formed a reversed-N shape but the shapely inter-wing I-struts were retained. The new centre section was constructed of riveted duralumin with steel tubular bars. The shape and size of the rudder were the only significant changes to the tail unit.

Many other structural items had to be strengthened to conform to the latest safety standards. For example, the fabric covering of the I-15's ailerons was replaced by duralumin and the front bracing wires were duplicated in tandem.

Wheel spats rigidly attached to the lower undercarriage fairings were fitted as standard along with wider 700 x 120 mm (27.5 x 4.7 in.) tyres and mechanically operated wheel brakes. As was customary with Soviet fighters of this era, skis could replace the wheels in harsh winters.

Above and below: '5 Red', a standard production I-15*bis* in green camouflage with pale blue undersurfaces.

Above and below: A still-unpainted I-15*bis* with the number '68' chalked on the rudder (possibly related to the c/n) undergoing trials.

Above: The moulded cockpit windshield of the I-15*bis*.

Above: The I-15*bis* could be equipped with skis for winter operations. Note the faired ski/landing gear axle attachment points and the tie-down lugs on the landing gear struts.

The spatted mainwheels of the I-15*bis*.

When required, RSI transceivers could now be installed, the electrical supply for which was taken from a dynamo.

The gun armament was still four synchronised 7.62-mm PV-1 machine-guns with 3,000 rounds in total and an OP-1 telescopic sight but the four DER-32 underwing bomb racks could now carry up to 150 kg (330 lb).

Production of the I-15*bis* totalled 2,408 examples, as follows:

	No. of Aircraft built at *zavod* 1
1937 and 1938	1,104
1939	1,304

Some sources give 1,301 for the 1939 production and a total of 2,405.

Data for a typical 1937-built I-15*bis* with M-25V engine:

Span	10.2 m (33.5 ft)
Length	6.2 m (20.3 ft)
Wing area	22.5 m² (242 sq. ft)
Weight:	
empty	1,243 kg (2,747 lb)
loaded	1,750 kg (3,859 lb)
Maximum speed:	
at sea level	321 km/h (199 mph)
at 3,500 m (11,480 ft)	370 km/h (230 mph)
Time to 5,000 m (16,400 ft),	6.75 minutes
Service ceiling	9,000 m (29,500 ft)
Time to complete 360° circle	11.0 seconds
Range	520 km (323 miles)
Take-off run	160 m (525 ft)
Landing speed	105 km/h (65 mph)

Operational history of the I-15*bis*

Units of the VVS began to receive the I-15*bis* in mid-1937 even before State Acceptance Trials had been passed. By this time reports of the success and popularity of the I-15 in the Spanish Civil War were putting pressure on the VVS High Command to justify their denigration of the I-15 by demonstrating the worth and superiority of its replacement, the I-15*bis*. The signing of the Sino-Soviet Non-Aggression Pact on 21st August 1937, with its secret clauses promising military aid to China, seemed to present a good opportunity for doing so. The second Sino-Japanese war had started on 7th July 1937 and so four 'volunteer' Soviet fighter squadrons were dispatched in November 1937 to the Nanking area to support the Chinese, with Stepan P. Sooproon as leader of the Soviet contingent. Their opponents were Imperial Japanese Army units equipped in the early stages with the Kawasaki Ki-10 biplanes, official designation Army Type 95 Model 1 (Allied code name 'Perry'), which were manufactured between

1935 and 1937. These were hopelessly out-classed by the Soviet aircraft and suffered heavy losses.

Disturbed by this setback, the Japanese High Command replaced the biplanes with the Mitsubishi A5M2a monoplane, Navy Type 96 Carrier Fighter Model 2-1 (Allied code name 'Claude') of the Imperial Navy. The monoplane, being faster, proved itself a match for the I-15*bis*, even though the biplane was more manoeuvrable and had the added advantages of twice as many machine-guns, a stronger structure and seat armour protection. In the face of these compensatory factors the outcome of battles between the two types hung on pilot skill and in this respect the two protagonists were well matched. However, the VVS decided to assess the I-16 against the newer Japanese fighters, and two I-15*bis* squadrons were replaced in January 1938 by two others equipped with I-16s.

The Chinese Air Force was also supplied with I-15*bis* fighters but in spite of Soviet help the training of pilots in general was poor and combat losses and accident attrition were very high. In all, two deliveries, totalling 186 of this type, were made to China in the first quarter of 1938 and equipped the 5th and 6th Fighter Groups, as well as serving in Soviet-staffed training schools. The Japanese response was to bring in Nakajima Ki-27, Army Type 97 Fighter (Allied code name 'Abdul') monoplanes to the China theatre of operations. On 15th April 12 Ki-10 biplanes and three Ki-27 monoplanes fought 30 Chinese-flown I-15*bis* and the Japanese claimed to have destroyed twenty-four without loss. The tables were turned on 29th April when a mixed force of two Chinese and four Soviet squadrons claimed the destruction of 36 out of 39 Japanese fighters for a loss of eleven of their own.

Stalin, at the end of 1938, personally authorised attrition replacements for the Spanish I-15s, signing an order for three consignments, each of thirty-one I-15*bis* aircraft, to be sent to help the Republican side. Of these, 62 were detained at the French border but the remaining 31 entered service in January 1939 after being assembled at Sabadell. A wing of three squadrons, each comprising nine aircraft, was formed with a further four fighters held as reserves. Overall command of the wing was given to Emilio Galera Macías who also had command of one of its three squadrons; the other two units were under the command of officers named Roderiguez and Mora. Although two machines were lost in training accidents, no combat losses were recorded. It has been said that the aircraft were used for ground strafing but the account cannot be substantiated because there were no reports of aerial combat. Towards the end of the war the twenty-nine surviving aero-

'Bail out!' This urgent message hastily painted on the fuselage of an I-15*bis* is conveyed to the pilot of an aircraft in trouble and lacking radio communication in a scene from a Soviet motion picture. The white side flash and 'racing number' on the tail may indicate that the fighter is operated by a display team.

This shot of an I-15bis ground-running its engine gives a good view of the cowling design.

Above: The pilot of a Soviet I-15*bis* reads a book between sorties (quite probably some propaganda literature or a field manual).

14 White, a Red Army Air Force I-15*bis*, prepares to take off on a sortie, toting four small bombs. Note the wheel spat attachment fittings on the wheel axles.

Above: 14 Red and 16 Red, a pair of I-15*bis* fighters wearing pre-war style insignia. Interestingly, both aircraft have a small red star on the fin.

This ski-equipped I-15*bis*, 11 White, was captured by the Finnish troops during the Winter War. The red star on the fuselage appears to be painted out.

Above: A captured I-15bis in full Finnish markings with the early-style 'war booty' serial VH-11 (VH stands for *vihollisen hävittäjä*, enemy fighter!). The aircraft is equipped with bomb racks, but the optical gunsight appears to be missing.

A slightly *decolleté* Finnish I-15bis in early-style markings, complete with yellow fuselage band; this aircraft was later reserialled IH-4. The dark-coloured tips of the upper wings are noteworthy.

Above: Another view of an *Ilmavoimat* I-15*bis* (the same aircraft as on the previous page).

A *Super Chato* captured by the Nationalists and wearing the early-style serial 2W-13.

planes flew to Carcassonne in France on 5th February.

In Spain, where it was known as the 'Super Chato', the I-15*bis* was deemed less manoeuvrable than the I-15, a deficit somewhat offset by the faster diving speed. This gave the potential of redressing the balance in any dogfight confrontations with the Italian-built Fiat C.R.32 fighter which had always been able to outdive the *Chato*. Republican I-15*bis* fighters were given three-digit registration numbers preceded by the letters 'CC'. Evidence suggests that the assembled aircraft were numbered CC-063 through CC-093, apparently indicating that they were from the third batch.

After the end of the Civil War about twenty I-15*bis* were returned by the French to the victorious Nationalist rebels and, serving as type 2W, formed *Grupo* 24, a part of the *Regimento Mixto de Caza Num* 23 at Reus in what became the *Ejercito del Aire*. In 1945 the type designation was changed to C9 and they served in the ground attack role until the mid-1940s.

The ill-defined Manchukuo-Mongolia border was disputed by the Japanese who, since 1936, had provoked skirmishes with Soviet-Mongolian forces along the Khalkhin-Gol River, skirmishes which escalated into a full-scale but undeclared war in 1939 when the Japanese appeared to be making preparations for an attack into Mongolia by outflanking the Soviet defences. The 'war' started on 11th May and continued until 16th September 1939. At first one regiment, the 70th IAP commanded by Major V. M. Zabalooyev and equipped primarily with the I-15*bis*, was in action together with the 22nd IAP and the I-16 monoplane. Another regiment equipped with the I-15*bis* and two more flying the I-16 later reinforced these units. Their enemy was mounted on the Nakajima Ki-27 monoplane that had previously fought against the Soviet volunteer squadrons in China. The Japanese fighter was superior to the Soviet monoplane in both manoeuvrability and rate of climb and

Top: More war booty. This ski-equipped I-15*bis* with the unusual three-digit serial '173 Yellow' was captured by the Finns in apparently perfect condition.

Centre: A Spanish I-15*bis* with post-war *Ejercito del Aire* markings (just visible beneath the lower wings) and bomb racks.

Bottom: Another I-15*bis* with post-war Spanish roundels on the fuselage (but not on the lower wings) and minus propeller spinner hangared at Reus where all *Super Chatos* captured by the Nationalists were based. Unusually, this one is still equipped with wheel spats; most *Super Chatos* supplied to Spain had the spats removed.

easily outpaced the biplanes in terms of speed. Huge air battles took place over the Nomonhan plateau, often involving up to two hundred aeroplanes, and wildly exaggerated claims were made by both sides.

It soon became clear that the I-15*bis*, even when protected by I-16s, was just not effective enough. Therefore thirteen of the newly-developed I-153 were tested in battle in a mixed regiment alongside 45 I-15*bis*. Not only new aircraft but also new weapons were employed in this conflict. Five of the I-15*bis* fighters were each fitted with six 82-mm RS-82 rockets for use against enemy aircraft. No information has been released of their success in destroying an enemy aeroplane but they were certainly extremely effective at dispersing enemy formations, allowing I-16s acting as top cover the opportunity to pick them off one at a time.

After the end of the conflict the Japanese at the time claimed to have destroyed 1,162 Soviet aeroplanes in the air and 98 on the ground; a total claim of 1,260 destroyed which is 2.5 times the total number of Soviet aircraft employed! To be fair, these claims have now been moderated to 400. Although Soviet claims were less wildly exaggerated, their claim of 590 in aerial victories and 55 on the ground was still in excess of the 500 aeroplanes being used by the Japanese. It is worth comparing admissions from both sides of their own losses; the Japanese own up to 154 lost or damaged beyond repair and the Soviets to 207. Most uncommitted observers would call the result of the aerial battle an honourable draw.

During the Winter War of 1939-40 with Finland, the VVS was not the only air force to operate the I-15*bis*. Five were captured by the Finns and served first in LeLv (*Lentolaivue*, squadron) 34, and later in 2/TLeLv 34, of the Finnish Air Force (*Ilmavoimat*) principally as fighter trainers and received serial numbers VH-1 through VH-5 (VH standing for *vihollisen hävittäjä* – enemy fighter), later becoming IH-1 through IH-5. They survived in this role into World War Two.

Operation *Barbarossa* opened on 22nd June 1941 with attacks on Soviet airfields during which many VVS regiments used a mix of the I-15*bis* and the I-153. Deliveries of the latter had begun in April 1941; the policy was to spread the available supply thinly over numerous units rather than thickly over a few. The 74th ShAP (*shtoormovoy aviatsionnyy polk* – attack regiment) was based only 14 km (8.6 miles) from the border and in the opening attack it lost all 47 aircraft on the airfield to artillery fire and bombs. Orders for the 66th and 164th IAPs to take off were received just before dawn on Day 1 but there was not enough time to achieve this before the bombs rained down, destroying 34 fighters, almost

Above: I-15*bis* '68 Yellow' equipped with rocket launch rails was captured by the Germans after force-landing on a road.

Above: A Chinese I-15*bis* serialled 305. The roundels are carried on the wings only and just about the only indication of the fighter's 'nationality' in this photo is the blue and white striped rudder.

This I-15*bis* is a development aircraft featuring a non-standard abbreviated NACA cowling.

Above: Head-on view of the supercharged I-15bisTK.

This view of the I-15bisTK shows the starboard exhaust-driven supercharger and the non-standard pointed spinner. The aircraft was mostly white and the cowling and wheel spats were painted red.

Above: This aircraft is possibly a pre-production I-15*bis*TK with the supercharger on the port side.

A flight of factory-fresh pre-production I-15*bis*TKs. The offset position of the air intake and the portside supercharger are clearly visible.

Above: An I-15*bis* with four underwing drop tanks.

Above: This I-15*bis* (possibly the same aircraft) carries an experimental centreline drop tank. Note the unusual colour scheme with silver dope applied over standard camouflage.

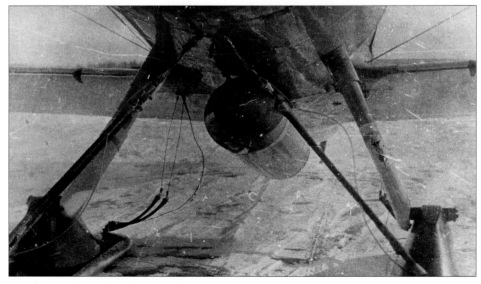

Close-up of the drop tank on the aircraft depicted above.

all of them I-15*bis*. Away to the south the 62nd IAP, reputed to be one of the best in the Kiev Special Military District, lost half its inventory.

On the southern flank, pilots of the 96th Independent Fighter Squadron were the first in the Black Sea Fleet Air Arm to engage the enemy. There were 14 I-15*bis* and three I-153s on strength and when their Romanian opponents attacked Izmail in the afternoon of 22nd June they were repulsed and the first blood fell to Lt M. Maksimov. Captain A. Korobitsin was the proud commander of this squadron, the first unit in the Soviet Navy to be awarded the Order of the Red Banner.

In the north, a ShAP commanded by Hero of the Soviet Union V. Belousov distinguished itself in the interceptor role when Captain M. Krasnolootskiy in his I-15*bis* rammed and destroyed a Messerschmitt Bf 109 and was still able to limp home. For this act of bravery he was awarded the Gold Star of the Hero of the Soviet Union.

As the war progressed, more modern Soviet fighters increasingly took over the interceptor role and the I-15*bis* moved on to ground attack in daylight and to supplementing the U-2 (Po-2LNB) night bombers. A good example of extemporisation in the field occurred when the 65th ShAP discovered that when rockets attached to the underside of the lower wings of the I-15*bis* were fired, fabric was stripped off the wing and its structure warped. Undaunted, the mechanics attached duralumin sheets to the wing undersides, reinforced the spars and fitted additional ribs. Bomb racks were also installed but the effect of the additional armament and the use of ski undercarriages reduced the top speed to 240 km/h (150 mph). These intrepid pilots needed to use all the excellent manoeuvrability of the biplane to avoid presenting an easy target for the Luftwaffe's 'Experten' in their Bf 109s.

Still in front-line service in summer 1943 several I-15*bis* used for artillery correction were given a second cockpit for an observer by regimental mechanics of the 5th Air Army.

I-15*bis*TK high-altitude fighter

A test aircraft with an M-25V motor was provided in 1939 with two TK superchargers driven by the engine exhaust via a divided pipe. Designated I-15*bis*TK (*s **toorbokompressorom** – supercharged), it was white overall except for the wheel spats and cowling, which were red, and photographs indicate that it carried no 'tactical number'. On test, its top speed at 6,000 km (19,700 ft) was a creditable 435 km/h (270 mph) but the extra weight of 140 kg (308 lb) degraded other aspects of the aircraft's performance and manoeuvrability. A small series of ten was built for use against the high-altitude reconnaissance aircraft and bombers (eg, Junkers Ju 86P) that the Germans were known to be developing.

I-15bisGK high-altitude fighter

During the period 29th August to 4th October 1939, a modified I-15bis designated I-15bisGK (s ghermeticheskoy kabinoy, with hermetically sealed cockpit) explored the potential of the latest pressure cabin designed by A. Ya. Schcherbakov. It was similar to that tested on an I-15 but the soft rubber which sealed the hemispherical duralumin cupola to the fuselage was given a rubberised fabric sheet as internal protection and a cotton wool layer as external protection. The semi-circular cupola now had nine glazed panels and the cabin itself was firmly attached to the framework of the fuselage. V. P. Fyodorov made seven flights, the last of these on 4th October 1939 ended with a taxying accident which halted the programme. The additional weight of 67 kg (148 lb), coupled with an inability to open the cupola at high speeds, led to the development of the I-15bisGK being stopped in spite of the pressure cabin itself being considered a success. However, further development of the cabin continued, using the I-153 fighter.

I-15bisDM (I-152DM?) development aircraft

I-15bis with construction number 5942 made a strong claim to fame in December 1939, when, with P. Ye. Loginov at the controls, it made the first-ever flight of a ramjet-equipped piloted aeroplane. Under each lower wing it carried a DM-2 ramjet (dopolnitel'nyy motor – supplementary motor) which had been developed by Ivan A. Merkoolov from the smaller DM-1; hence the aircraft was known as the I-15bisDM. These engines had a diameter of 400 mm (15 3/4 in.), a length of 1.5 m (4.92 ft), a thrust of 0.187 kN (42 lb st) and ran on the same fuel as the piston engine. The first five flights were used to test and perfect the in-flight starting procedure. Subsequent flights recorded the increase in speed with ramjets engaged and were used to devise methods of reducing the starting-up time and to test improvements made to the combustion process. An increase in maximum speed of approximately 22 km/h (14 mph) was recorded and tests continued until May 1940, by which time 54 flights had been successfully completed. Sources are equally divided as to whether or not this modified I-15bis aircraft was redesignated I-152DM on completion.

I-15bis 'survivors'

No genuine example of the I-15bis exists today but there are three replicas. Details are given in the table on this page.

DIT-2 fighter trainer

During the summer of 1939 a two-seat trainer version of the I-15bis designated DIT-2 (dvookhmesnyy istrebitel' trenirovochnyy –

Above: The I-15bisDM (also referred to as the I-152DM) was a development aircraft equipped with two Merkoolov DM-2 ramjet boosters under the lower wings.

Another view of the I-15bisDM (I-152DM), showing the special fittings attaching the boosters to the lower wings.

Markings/tactical number	Location	Notes
Red Army Air Force / '50 White'	Central Russian Air Force Museum, Monino near Moscow	Replica for static display
Red Army Air Force / '14 White'	Central Museum of the Great Patriotic War, Moscow	Replica for static display
Red Army AF / '7 Red' with white outline, registered RA-02915 and named 'Yelena' when displayed at the MAKS-2001 airshow (14-19th August 2001); reregistered FLA RF-02915* during the show!	Sold to private owner in the USA (via Alpine Fighter Collection, New Zealand)	Rebuilt to flying condition by Rosaero Ltd and Aviarestavratsiya LLC at NAPO** from wreck found 1997 in northern Karelia; ASh-62IR engine, non-authentic propeller and tailwheel instead of tailskid

*FLA RF = Federahtsiya lyubiteley aviahtsi Rosseeyskoy Federahtsii – Aviation Enthusiasts' Federation of the Russian Federation, an organisation which unites both homebuilders, owner-operators of production light aircraft and, to a certain extent, air clubs (those which are not in the framework of the ROSTO paramilitary sports/technical society).
**NAPO = Novosibeerskoye aviatsionnoye proizvodstvennoye ob"yedineniye – Novosibirsk Aircraft Production Association named after Valeriy P. Chkalov (former zavod No. 153).

Above : The DIT-2 trainer derivative of the I-15*bis* during manufacturer's flight tests. As per Polikarpov custom, the prototype received a smart red and white colour scheme but the 'dragon's back' shape of the colour division line was rather unusual.

Three-quarters rear view of the DIT-2 prototype, showing to advantage the tandem cockpits.

Above: The DIT-2 at NII VVS during State Acceptance Trials. Note that the aircraft wears a different colour scheme, the prevailing colour being light grey; the cowling is now grey, the wheel spats painted differently, and the rear cockpit windshield appears to have a different shape as well! This is very probably a different aircraft from the one on the previous page.

Rear view of the DIT-2. Stephen King's Langoliers have been at work here! Seriously, the white blotches are buildings or other aircraft in the background which have been retouched away for security reasons.

two-seat fighter trainer) was evaluated, the additional cockpit having a full set of controls. Only two prototypes (some sources state one) were completed at *zavod* 1, the overall dimensions remaining the same as the single-seater's. Like many I-15*bis* test aircraft, the first prototype was painted white with red wheel spats and cowling but no identification number.

Although other aspects of stability and controllability were adequate, the DIT-2 was deemed unacceptable as a trainer because of its unsatisfactory spinning characteristics resulting from the changed centre of gravity. In spite of the removal of the backrest armour and two machine-guns with their ammunition the second cockpit added 52 kg (114 lb) to the weight, and that was before adding the weight of the extra crew member.

I-152 single-seat fighter prototypes
It had been intended that the production standard-setter for the I-15*bis* in 1938 would be redesignated I-152 and have the following alterations:

- the engine exhaust manifolds replaced by individual stacks for each cylinder to reduce weight;

- self-sealing fuel tanks;

- two sets of shock absorbers for the engine to reduce vibrations;

- a Townend type cowling to replace the larger NACA cowling;

- a pneumatic starter for the engine replacing the Hucks starter dog;

- an optically flat panel in the windscreen to reduce distortions.

Tests with the prototype (construction number 3495) showed insignificant differences when compared with series aircraft and there was also concern about the effect of using individual exhaust stacks at night, therefore VVS instructed *zavod* 1 to continue producing the I-15*bis*. Although not commented upon at the time, the start of production in 1939 of the new gull-winged I-153 must have affected this VVS decision.

The above information was obtained from Russian State Military Archives (RGVA f. 24708 op. 8 d. 603).

Dimensions were the same as for the I-15bis and the following additional data was obtained from the prototype I-152, in its successful State Acceptance Tests which took place from 3rd June to 29th July 1938 (see also RGVA f. 24708 op. 9 d. 150 and 574):

Basic specifications of the I-152

Weight, loaded	1,648 kg (3,634 lb)
Maximum speed:	
at sea level	325 km/h (202 mph)
at 3,200 m (10,500 ft)	367 km/h (228 mph)
Time to 5,000 m (16,400 ft)	7.3 minutes
Service ceiling	9,000 m (29,500 ft)
Time to complete 360° circle	11.0 seconds
Landing speed	105 km/h (65 mph)

Further tests with a new VISh-6A variable-pitch propeller showed an improved service ceiling of 9,600 m (31,500 ft).

I-152TK
A few sources refer to the I-15*bis* M-25V tested with a TK-1 turbocharger as the I-152TK but this is unlikely to be the correct designation.

I-152DM or I-15*bis*DM
Sources are equally divided as to whether or not the modified I-15*bis* aircraft construction number 5942 was redesignated I-152DM on being fitted with two underwing DM-2 ramjets. Details of its successful flight in December 1939 are included under I-15*bis*DM.

I-15*bis* fighters in various stages of disassembly undergoing refurbishment at a Red Army Air Force aircraft repair workshop sometime in the late 1930s. '16 White' appears to have flipped over on landing. The nearest aircraft is stripped down completely, revealing the primary fuselage truss.

Chapter 5

The Return of the Gull

I-153 Chaika single-seat fighter (*tip* 34)

Neither the military nor Polikarpov were happy with the performance of the I-15*bis*, and the question of its successor was one of the issues debated at a meeting in July 1937 chaired by Stalin at which the lessons of the Spanish Civil War were to be taken into account. It was alleged that the Fiat C.R.32 biplane was superior to the I-16 monoplane and so the policy of the VVS having a mixed force of biplane and monoplane fighters was continued. No account was taken of the obvious (to the outside world anyway) superiority of the Messerschmitt Bf 109 over both types.

Polikarpov did not try to discourage this loyalty to biplanes – perhaps because he was also the designer of the current Soviet monoplane and wanted to design both types. Instead he concentrated on trying to break the vicious circle of increasing speed by installing a more powerful engine which then adversely affected weight and therefore manoeuvrability. He indicated ways of minimising drag and structural weight so that he could still install the most powerful engine available whilst retaining an acceptable level of manoeuvrability. His solution included reverting to the gull-wing layout for the upper wings and fitting a retractable undercarriage.

The People's Commissariat of the Defence Industry (Narkomoboronprom) and the VVS accepted Polikarpov's thesis, no doubt strongly influenced by favourable comments reaching the USSR from pilots using the I-15 in Spain. Only slightly less influential was the favourable report from TsAGI show-

Above: The first prototype of the I-153 (c/n 5001) seen in the autumn of 1938.

Centre and immediately above: Two views of the same aircraft prior to painting. Note the open front of the engine cowling without cooling shutters.

Above: The second prototype I-153 ('5 Red', c/n 6005) powered by an M-25V engine had an overall silver colour scheme.

A side view of the second prototype. Like the first prototype, it had a large I-16-style propeller spinner which was not used on production examples.

The second prototype I-153 trestled for landing gear retraction tests. Note how the mainwheels rotate around the legs during retraction.

ing that, with the gull-wing configuration, directional stability actually improved as speed increased. This sudden change of heart by the VVS staff may have been, on the one hand, a conviction in the strength of the arguments but on the other, could be attributable to the fact that the officers in charge felt safe in making a *volte-face* because they had not condemned the I-15 in the first place. Those who had done so may have been purged for other reasons.

On 13th October 1937, preliminary design details were submitted and the formal go-ahead for the new biplane fighter was given ten days later. Confident of the outcome, Polikarpov had already asked his deputy Dmitriy L. Tomashevich to start work on the design and the detail design work was given to Aleksandr Ya. Schcherbakov. The fighter was designated I-153 by the VVS and, as some sources suggest, I-15*ter* (*ter* being an abbreviation of the Latin for 'third', *tertius*) by the OKB; an assertion that it also had the designation TsKB-3*ter* seems improbable as TsKB GUAP no longer existed. Apart from the gull-like formation of its upper wings, the I-153 was structurally similar to the I-15*bis* but a manually operated retractable undercarriage with wider tyres was installed and a tailwheel replaced the movable skid. It had been intended to use the M-62 from the start of series production but it was not available in time, so the M-25V was substituted at first. Not unexpectedly the aircraft became known as Chaika (Seagull).

When the design of the I-153 had been approved Polikarpov was in charge of OKBs at two factories. One of them, *zavod* 84 at Khimki, was becoming involved with trans-

port aircraft and would later produce the Douglas DC-3 under licence as the PS-84 (Lisunov Li-2). The other, *zavod* 21 in Gor'kiy, was just building up its experimental facilities as well as mass-producing the I-16 and so the obvious choice for the preparation of working drawings fell upon *zavod* 1 which had been selected to manufacture the I-153. Unfortunately this plant was struggling to start series production of the I-15*bis* and at the same time improve its own unsatisfactory quality performance. Inevitably there was a delay of several months before the drawings could be started and they were not completed until May 1938. It was only then that construction of the prototypes was able to begin.

Polikarpov was no longer involved with plants 21 and 84 from December 1937 onwards. He had been transferred to ZOK (*Zavod opytnykh konstrooktsiy*), the experimental design plant of TsAGI in Moscow; on 30th December 1936 ZOK was redesignated *zavod* 156. Being successful enough to be called 'the King of Fighters' had made many people envious of Polikarpov, an envy exacerbated by Stalin's apparent patronage. The shunting from plant to plant that he and his team were now subjected to has been interpreted by many as a vindictive manoeuvre to clear the path for his ambitious, if so far less successful, younger rival designers of fighters.

The first prototype of the I-153 (construction number 5001) was built with a 750-hp (560-kW) M-25V engine and made its first flight in August 1938, piloted by Aleksandr I. Zhookov. Factory tests, which took place between 27th September and 5th October, showed a number of defects, lack of rigidity in the wings, aileron vibration and tail unit jolting

being the most serious. Whilst the test results were not acceptable, it was decided not to hold up production. Most faults were corrected on a pre-production batch of ten which was completed in October at *zavod* 1 with M-25V engines driving fixed-pitch propellers with large spinners. These aircraft received elevators reduced in surface area, a strengthened undercarriage, fuel tank protection and an improved control system. A batch of five (c/ns 6002, 6004, 6008, 6009, 6010) was sent to Baku in the Republic of Azerbaijan for testing in a more amenable climate from 25th February to 20th March 1939. State Acceptance Tests also took place there on the second prototype I-153 M-25V ('5 Red', c/n 6005) from 20th March and were successfully completed on 15th June 1939 by test pilot Pavel Ya. Fedrovi with a comment that the jolting had not yet been completely overcome and a complaint about the poor view of the ground from the cockpit. Performance results from 454 flights were satisfactory, with a maximum speed of 424 km/h (264 mph) at 3,500 m (11,500 ft), a service ceiling of 8,700 m (28,500 ft), a time to 5,000 m (16,400 ft) of 6.4 minutes and the ability to perform a 360° turn in under 12 seconds.

There was, however, a tragic accident on 11th April 1939 which destroyed I-153 M-25V c/n 6008 when the aircraft broke up in the air following the failure of its wing structure on pulling out of a 500 km/h (311 mph) dive. NII VVS pilots subsequently performed more than 1,500 aerobatic manoeuvres in an I-153 (c/n 6540) to prove its durability.

Between 16th June and 16th August 1939, State Acceptance Tests were carried out on another I-153 prototype (c/n 6019) with an

Above: This M-63 powered I-153 (c/n 6931) was the *etalon* (production standard-setter) for 1940. Note the larger carburettor air intake atop the cowling and the aerial mast on top of the starboard upper wing.

A side view of the 1940 *etalon*. The skis were fully retractable; note the connecting rods ahead of the main gear struts which rotated the skis parallel to the fuselage waterline during gear retraction/extension.

A three-quarters rear view of the M-63 powered I-153 c/n 6931.

800-hp (597-kW) M-62 engine and fixed-pitch propeller with a large spinner. The engine had recently been developed by A. D. Shvetsov from the M-25V by fitting it with a two-stage supercharger, a new induction system, as well as numerous other improvements. A maximum speed of 443 km/h (275 mph) at 4,600 m (15,100 ft) was recorded, together with a service ceiling of 9,800 m (29,900 ft), and it took 13 seconds to complete a 360° turn. The tests were considered unsuccessful, insufficient maximum speed being quoted as the reason for its failure. The disappointing results were a little embarrassing, to say the least, because not only had production already begun but also the variant had even received its baptism of fire against the Japanese in Mongolia. Whilst in Mongolia, trials were conducted in service conditions with various types of fixed and variable-pitch propellers. As a result of these and other trials the AV-1 variable-pitch prop was made standard equipment for the I-153 M-62 and normally no spinner was fitted. State Acceptance Tests of the I-153 M-62 were not fully completed until 17th January 1941 when aircraft No. 6566 passed all the tests, including that for safe recovery from a spin.

During 1940 the M-62 engine, in its turn, was replaced on the production lines of *zavod* 1 by the more powerful 900-hp (671-kW) M-63

with the AV-1 propeller; at first no spinners were fitted but later series had small spinners. Two prototypes (c/ns 6012 and 6039) had left the factory in 1939 for engine tests. Any expected improvement in maximum speed was, however, negated by extra equipment and further reinforcements to the structure but the rate of climb was considerably enhanced. State Acceptance Tests of this variant, the so-called '1940 *etalon*' (production standard-setter), were completed on 30th September 1939 by the aircraft with c/n 6931.

Because the M-62 and M-63 engines were heavier than the M-25V, more problems were encountered on recovery from a spin. On the third spiral a flat spin was induced, followed by engine cut-out on the fifth spiral. The aircraft recovered from the spin by itself on the tenth or twelfth spiral and on diving the engine restarted. Trials were conducted in spring 1939 with I-153 M-62 c/n 6019 and then with I-153 M-63, c/n 8019, in June and July 1940, resulting in a new procedure for training service pilots in spin recovery by confining the flights to above 5,000 m (16,400 ft) and limiting the manoeuvre to two spirals.

Another problem occurred with the M-63 when, as a result of engine cut-out and even sometimes destruction through overheating, all I-153 and I-16 aircraft with the M-63 were grounded for about three months, starting on

31st August 1940. The cause was traced to supercharger overheating during take-off and at other times when maximum power was used; accordingly a procedure was developed to enable the pilot to avoid this problem by different use of the controls.

Structural description of the I-153

Apart from the gull-like formation of the upper wings, the structure of the I-153 was very similar to that of the I-15bis, with Clark YH airfoils, fabric covered wings with wooden spars but the same steel structure as on the I-15 to integrate the upper wings into the fuselage

The fuselage of the I-153 differed from that of the I-15bis only in having a more circular cross-section. It retained the main frame made of welded KhMA steel tubes with L-shaped sections of rolled duralumin added as a secondary structure to form the streamlined shape. Removable D1 duralumin panels covered the nose as far back as the cockpit and doped linen fabric covered the rear fuselage with double seam lacing and calico strips. The tail unit remained unchanged. Inside the cockpit, the pilot's seat was given a 9 mm (0.35 in.) thick armoured back.

The main undercarriage was the most innovative part of the aircraft and consisted of an oleo-pneumatic leg braced laterally by a diagonal strut; both leg and strut pivoted to

Above: Close-up of the engine cowling, showing the cooling shutter and the AV-1 propeller's hub design.
Below: A PAU-22 gun camera could be installed between the upper wings.

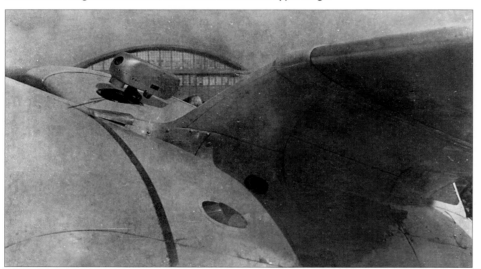

Close-up of the retractable skis, showing the torque links and telescopic rotation links. The photo was taken after a malfunction; the arrows show where the axle had jammed and hydraulic fluid had leaked out.

the rear during retraction and plates attached to the leg struts formed covers for the under-carriage. The wheels rotated through 90° to lie flat in a well on the underside of the wing roots. Retraction was manually operated via a cockpit handcrank. Problems were expected with the new undercarriage system but tests showed it to be reliable, even if it must have been difficult for the pilots to operate whilst wearing bulky winter flying suits. Tyres were now wider at 700 mm x 150 mm (27.5 x 4.7 in.) and a solid-tyred tailwheel moving in syn-chronisation with the rudder replaced the tail-skid. Equipment included a battery, an engine-driven dynamo, navigation lights and provision for a radio.

Three types of engines were used to power the I-153:

- the 750-hp (560-kW) M-25V with a fixed-pitch propeller and large spinner was used initially because the preferred M-62 was not available in time. The M-25V was developed from the Wright Cyclone SGR-1820-F3 and produced 775 hp for take-off. Total about ten aircraft;

- the 800-hp (597-kW) M-62 with an AV-1 propeller, a refined version of the M-25V with a two-stage supercharger and improved induction system; it produced 1,000 hp (746 kW) for take-off and 800 hp (596 kW) at 2,900 m (9,500 ft). Spinners were not fitted as standard with the M-62 engine. Total about 3,018 aircraft;

- the 900-hp (671-kW) M-63 with an AV-1 propeller was a further development of the M-62, producing 1,100 hp (821 kW) for take-off and 900 hp (671 kW) at 4,500 m (14,800 ft). Small spinners were fitted as standard. Total 409 aircraft.

Cowlings were shorter than those used on the I-15*bis*, with apertures for individual cylin-der exhaust pipes and an air intake duct for the carburettor on the top.

Starting in March 1939, experiments were conducted to determine the best type of external fuel tank. Both I-153 and I-15*bis* air-craft were used in the trials. At first cylindrical metal tanks, each holding 150 litres (33 gal.), were carried under the fuselage, then teardrop-shaped metal tanks carried under the lower wings were tried. The latter were adopted; at first the fighters carried two 50-litre (11 gal.) tanks under each wing, giving 200 litres (44 gal.) more fuel. When an extra 25-litre (5.5 gal.) oil tank was also installed the aircraft's range could be doubled. After exten-sive experimentation the decision was taken to standardise on two 100-litre (22-gal.) fibre underwing drop tanks. These tanks were car-ried by both I-153 and I-16.

The armament was improved over the I-15*bis* on even the lightest armed variant by replacing the four PV-1 machine-guns, each firing 750 rounds per minute and weighing

14.5 kg (32.0 lb), with four ShKAS firing 1,800 rounds per minute and weighing only 10.6 kg (23.4 lb). Most aircraft carried 2,500 rounds of ammunition but those with M-25V engines had only 2,300 rounds. Four underwing bomb racks could now carry up to 200 kg (441 lb), exceeding the maximum bomb load of the I-15*bis*, which was 150 kg (330 lb).

In August 1939 an I-153 M-62 (c/n 6021) was armed with two 12.7-mm (.50 calibre) TKB-150 machine-guns. Each had only 165 rounds but could be reloaded in flight, using compressed air. These new machine-guns were also in great demand for the army and in such short supply that it was decided to fit only one, together with two ShKAS 7.62-mm machine-guns, until more were available. This armament combination was tested on aircraft c/n 6506 in February and March 1940 and in the autumn at the Kubinka gunnery range on aircraft c/ns 8527, 8528 and 8545, eventually being incorporated into some 150 I-153 M-62s built by *zavod* 1 that year. By now, further developed by N. Ye. Berezin, the new gun was in production as the UBS (*ooniver-sahl'nyy* [*poolemyot*] *Berezina sinkhronnyy*, versatile Berezin [machine-gun], synchronised), but this was usually abbreviated to BS.

Trials of aircraft with 20-mm cannons are described under I-153P.

From the second half of 1940, following the successful use of RS-82 rockets in the Khalkhin-Gol campaign, provisions for fitting removable RO-82 rocket launch rails were made to new aircraft. Over 400 I-153s had been thus modified by the end of 1940.

In all, 3,437 I-153s were manufactured over a four-year period, as illustrated in the table at the head of page 86.

In spite of sporting skis and being 122 kg (270 lb) heavier, the M-63 powered I-153 was slightly faster than the version with the M-62 engine and had a much better rate of climb.

Operational history of the I-153

A mystery clouds the beginnings of the service career of the I-153. Did any serve with the Republican forces in Spain? Some Spanish sources suggest that one or two aircraft were tested there by Soviet pilots towards the end of 1938 but no firm evidence has been offered. The authenticity of the story relies upon the appearance in France during the war of the I-153 which now graces the *Musée de l'Air et de l'Espace* in Paris but it has also been suggested that this aircraft was taken there by the Germans to show off as a war trophy.

Deliveries to the VVS began in October 1938 when five I-153s with M-25V engines were sent to Baku for service testing. Training units were the next recipients. A. D. Loktionov, the VVS Commander, ordered that the first operational unit to receive them should be the

Above: The M-25V engine of the second prototype with the NACA cowling removed. The cylinder heads are marked *Zavod No.19* (the engine's manufacturer). The barrels of the machine-guns are also visible.

Above: The windshield and the PAK-1 collimator gunsight.

Close-up of the second prototype's main undercarriage units with the rear wheel well doors in place.

Секретно.

Above: I-153 c/n 8019 powered by an M-63 engine with an AV-1 was used for spinning trials in June-July 1940. Note the small pointed spinner sometimes fitted to production Chaikas.

Test equipment sensors were attached to the tail surfaces of I-153 c/n 8019 to record rudder and elevator deflection during spin recovery.

Above: I-153 c/n 6566 was also used for spinning tests. Note how the wheel wells have been almost entirely faired over, leaving only small recesses for the upper parts of the skis. The aircraft was presumably dark red overall except for the natural metal cowling.

Unlike I-153 c/n 8019, no test equipment sensors were apparent on c/n 6566. The position of the star insignia on the tail is unusual for the pre-war period.

No. of Aircraft built at zavod 1 imeni Aviakhima			
M-25V	M-62	M-63	Totals
1938-9	10	988	13	1011
1940		2030	332	2362
1941			64	64
Totals	10	3018	409	3437

Basic specifications of the I-153

Construction number	6005 (second prototype)	6062 (production)	6540 (production) with skis
Powerplant	M-25V with fixed-pitch propeller	M-62 with AV-1 variable-pitch propeller	M-63 with AV-1 variable-pitch propeller
Span	10.0 m (32.8 ft)	10.0 m (32.8 ft)	10.0 m (32.8 ft)
Length	6.17 m (20.2 ft)	6.17 m (20.2 ft)	6.17 m (20.2 ft)
Wing area	22.14 m² (238 sq. ft)	22.14 m² (238 sq. ft)	22.14 m² (238 sq. ft)
Weight:			
empty	n.a.	1,375 kg (3,031 lb)	n.a.
loaded	1,680 kg (3,704 lb)	1,765 kg (3,891 lb)	1,887 kg (4,161 lb)
Maximum speed:			
at sea level	368 km/h (229 mph)	366 km/h (227 mph)	370 km/h (230 mph)
at 5,000 m (16,400 ft)	412 km/h (256 mph)	425 km/h (264 mph)	428 km/h (266 mph)
at 7,000 m (22,970 ft)	376 km/h (234 mph)	408 km/h (254 mph)	401 km/h (249 mph)
Climb time:			
to 5,000 m	6.48 minutes	5.5 minutes	5.1 minutes
to service ceiling	27.4 minutes	31.0 minutes	24.5 minutes
Service ceiling	8,700 m (28,500 ft)	11,000 m (36,100 ft)	10,600 m (35,800 ft)
Range	n.a.	560 km (348 miles)	n.a.
Time to complete 360° circle	11 seconds	13 seconds	14 seconds
Take-off run	200 m (656 ft)	106 m (348 ft)	129 m (423 ft)
Landing run	n.a.	150 m (492 ft)	n.a.
Landing speed	n.a.	105 km/h (65 mph)	n.a.

22nd IAP in Mongolia, which was given 13 as replacements for some I-15bis fighters. Hero of the Soviet Union Sergey I. Gritsevets led a special group flying the I-153 and was delighted with the performance of his new mounts but horrified to find the synchronisation gear was broken on all of them. Fortunately this discovery happened during ground firing tests and a new fire control system was quickly devised and installed by regimental engineers.

For their first mission on 7th July 1939, nine of these fighters were deployed with undercarriages deliberately left unretracted in the hope that the enemy would be lulled into a false sense of security by perceiving the I-153 as the I-15bis, which, it was well known, had significantly inferior performance. A similar number of Nakajima Ki-27 monoplanes dived to attack from the rear and just before they came within gun range Gritsevets gave the signal for the undercarriages of the I-153s to be retracted and as the biplanes accelerated they quickly turned through 180° and

mounted a frontal attack. The ruse was successful and four Japanese fighters were immediately destroyed; the rest turned tail and made for home. There were no losses on the Soviet side. Japanese sources only admit to two losses. However, once enemy pilots had discovered the strengths and weaknesses of the I-153 they devised new tactics to avoid close combat and losses in the biplane units steadily grew. To be effective it was necessary that the I-153 go into battle with I-16 monoplanes as top cover.

A total of 70 I-153s were sent to Mongolia equipping the 22nd, 56th and 70th IAPs. These included 13 22nd IAP aircraft with M-62 engines whose performance was carefully monitored to enable any faults to be discovered and corrected. One example (c/n 6071) had a VV-1 variable-pitch propeller (VV = vozdooshnyy vint, airscrew) and the other 12 fixed-pitch propellers. Operations reached a peak between 9th August and 6th September, during which period up to six sorties per day were flown by each pilot. Losses of the

Chaika amounted to 23 aircraft from 28th July to 15th September 1939.

Operations in Mongolia revealed the Chaika to have structural weaknesses and more firing mechanism defects, both of which were first put right in the field and then on the production lines. The main problem, however, was the unreliability of the M-62 engines which needed changing every 60-80 hours because of supercharger failures. An unexpected worry was the strong air draught into the cockpit from the wheel wells fanning any fire that started, thus putting the pilot at risk of incineration. The propeller test gave interesting results: performances were similar, except that the variable-pitch propeller improved take-off time but seriously reduced range.

The result of the Khalkhin-Gol campaign was a tactical victory for the Soviet General (later Marshal) Gheorgiy K. Zhookov, whose forces virtually annihilated the Japanese 6th Army. More importantly, it was a great strategic victory in that the Japanese lost the urge to expand into Mongolia and did not attack even when the USSR was at its weakest and the Wehrmacht at the gates of Moscow. Stalin was able to transfer army divisions from the now less vulnerable Far Eastern sector and employ them in the defence of Moscow and later Stalingrad. Another result of this victory was that, having decided not to attack the USSR, the Japanese expanded to the south, thus bringing the USA into the war.

Chaikas were used extensively during the Winter War with Finland and, according to Finnish claims, suffered heavy losses along with the other Soviet types. Eight I-153 fighters that had engaged in this war and a further three in the Continuation War, all of which had made forced landings in Finland, were repaired and used by the Ilmavoimat together with eleven captured by the Germans in Russia and sold to the Finns. These aircraft formed Flight 3 of LeLv 6 providing fighter escort for the maritime patrol unit. In November 1942 the Chaikas became Flight 2 of LeLv 30. All were withdrawn from service on 20th March 1944. The serials VH-11 to VH-31 were given to 21 of these fighters which were later renumbered IT-11 to IT-31. Five Soviet aircraft were claimed to have been destroyed for the loss of two Finnish I-153s in combat and two in accidents.

Another country to receive the I-153, this time with the agreement of the Soviets, was China. Soviet aid to Chiang Kai-Shek was on a much larger scale than generally credited in the West as 1,250 aircraft were supplied between 1937 and early 1941. Of these, 93 were Chaikas and they formed three Groups located near large cities for their air defence. Unfortunately many were flown by inadequately trained Chinese pilots without much success against Japanese Ki-27s.

Above and below: A silver-doped M-63 engined I-153 on skis. Note the difference in colour between the areas skinned in metal and fabric.

Above: A pair of I-153s of the Red Banner Baltic Fleet Air Arm's 71st IAP taxies out for a sortie, armed with eight RS-82 rockets each. '102 White' in the background, the mount of Major Biskoop, is wearing non-standard three-tone camouflage; note the wartime location of the national insignia and serial.

'3 Red', an I-153 with quadruple RO-82 launch rails under the lower wings, was one of the many Soviet aircraft captured or destroyed by the Germans in the opening days of the Great Patriotic War. Note the missing skin panel near the cockpit.

Above: A pair of Chaikas toting four small bombs each, take off on a ground attack sortie. '24 White' in the foreground displays its starboard side for comparison with the port side shown opposite.

I-153s on an improvised airstrip. The aft gear door segments attached to the main gear struts were often removed in service for much the same reasons as the wheel spats on the I-15/I-15bis.

Above: A Soviet pilot runs for his aircraft past an I-153 serialled '7 Red' during an alert in the winter of 1941-42.

Cranking up the engine of an I-153 serialled '5 Yellow' at an airfield near Nikolayev on the Southern Front with the help of a GAZ-AA 1.5-ton truck equipped with the Hucks starter system, August 1941.

Above: Caught by the camera seconds before getting airborne, this Chaika operated by the 7th IAP (Leningrad Front) wears very non-standard camouflage, probably applied in field conditions.

'10 White', a Naval Air Arm I-153, parked under camouflage netting; the pilot, Lieutenant V. Red'ko, stands beside, ready to take off at short notice, September 1941.

Above: A Finnish Air Force pilot of 3/LeLV 6 poses beside his I-153 (IT-16/'5 Yellow'). He should know better than to leave the aircraft unoccupied with the engine running and no chocks!

IT-2/'7 White', another *Ilmavoimat* I-153, in dark green/black camouflage with yellow fuselage band.

Above: This ski-equipped I-153 entered Finnish service on 18th April 1940 with the 'war booty' serial VH-101. The fighter retains Soviet olive green camouflage with pale blue undersurfaces. It was subsequently reserialled VH-11 and then IT-11, eventually being destroyed in a landing accident on 24th February 1945.

One more Finnish I-153 with bomb racks.

Above: An unserialled Chinese I-153 in overall dark green finish. The fighter carries only roundels on the lower wings. The propeller is missing (the picture was possibly taken during reassembly after delivery).

Above: This Chinese Chaika has more complete national insignia with a blue and white striped rudder. The serial P-7250 is probably derived from the aircraft's c/n.

Ilmavoimat I-153 VH-13 after nosing over on landing. Talk about unlucky numbers! The patches in the middle of the Finnish roundels on the wings are noteworthy.

When the Germans attacked the Soviet Union on 22nd June 1941, over one third of the Soviet fighters confronting them in the Western sector of the USSR were I-153s. There were 179 in the Leningrad Military District in the 7th, 19th, 26th, 153rd and 154th IAPs. In the Baltic Military District 284 Chaikas served with the 15th, 21st, 38th, 42nd, 49th and 148th IAPs. The Odessa Military District had 143 of them in the 4th and 55th IAPs. The Western Military District had 241 serving with the 122nd, 123rd, 127th and 129th IAPs. But by far the greatest concentration of Chaikas was in the Kiev Military District where there were no fewer than 454 in the 12th, 20th, 23rd, 46th, 91st, 92nd, 149th, 164th and 165th IAPs. Thus 1,301 I-153s were assigned to fighter regiments on this front. In addition, about 180 I-153s served in ground attack regiments Nos. 61, 62, 66, 74, 241 and 299 alongside the I-15*bis*. A grand total of nearly 1,500 Chaikas out of the 4,226 fighters were deployed in this sector.

Figures for the Naval Air Arm showed 687 I-15*bis* and I-153 biplanes on its inventory at this time out of a total of 763 aircraft (ie, 90%). Not all had yet been assigned to active Fleet regiments which had in total 148 I-15*bis* and 202 I-153s. Of the latter the Northern Fleet had 18 with the 177th IAP and 72nd SAP (***sme-shannyy aviatsionnyy polk*** – Composite Air Regiment); the Black Sea Fleet had 76 with the 8th, 9th and 32nd APs and the Baltic Fleet 108 with the 71st IAP and 12th, 13th and 104th OAPs (**ot*del'nyy aviatsionnyy polk*** – Independent Air Regiment).

In addition to the first-line units in the west the I-153 served with flying schools, reserve regiments and in Military Districts in other parts of the Soviet Union, particularly in the Far East.

The first day of Operation *Barbarossa* saw huge losses inflicted on the VVS by the Luftwaffe. As recounted earlier, all of the 74th ShAP's aircraft were destroyed, a similar fate befell the 66th ShAP, and the 62nd ShAP lost half its inventory. One regiment not taken unawares was the 127th IAP at Avgustovo, commanded by Lt Col. Gordiyenko, who by camouflaging and dispersing his aircraft succeeded in losing none. Two of his pilots, Lt S. Zhukovskiy and Senior Political Instructor A. Artem'yev, flew nine sorties each that day and shot down a total of seven enemy aircraft. Fighters from the 122nd IAP joined the 127th in the fray and together they destroyed 35 enemy machines on the first day.

Major Soorin, commander of the 123rd IAP, claimed the first Bf 109 at 0500 hrs and at 0800 hrs Captain Mozhayev leading his flight of four surprised another group of Messerschmitts and shot down three for the loss of one of their own. This unit based at Stigovo destroyed 30 enemy aircraft and lost nine.

In spite of these and similar heroic actions, the VVS fleet was decimated, with over 700 aircraft of all types being lost. The Luftwaffe continued to attack airfields and by the end of June the Western Front of the Soviet Armies had lost 1,200 aeroplanes out of a possible 1,900. These attacks were not mounted with impunity and up to 5th July 1941 the Soviets claimed the destruction of over 800 German machines; of these the lion's share fell to I-153s. Thanks to their military success in Mongolia in 1939 the Soviets were able to rush reinforcements from the Far East, among which was the 29th 'Red Banner' IAP with a mixed bag of I-153s and I-16s. After giving cover to the arrival by train of 29th Army soldiers as they, too, rallied to defend Smolensk, the regiment carried out low-level attacks on the advancing enemy. Its first aerial victory fell to Lt (jg) Youkhimovich who intercepted and shot down a Junkers Ju 88.

One incident displaying a tenacious defiance of danger deserves a place in any book of heroic ventures; Captain Tormorov and Lt (jg) Doodin were patrolling in the Velikiye Luki area, which necessitated the carriage of drop tanks, when they came under attack from four Bf 109s. Doodin shot one down but Tormovov's port drop tank was set on fire. He dived away to jettison it and the remaining three Bf 109s concentrated on Doodin. Tormorov, after succeeding in jettisoning his drop tanks, returned to the attack and shot down another and was able to return to base. Doodin went on to down a third by ramming it head-on and managed to parachute safely onto the Russian lines. It later transpired, when the wreckage was found, that they had also destroyed the fourth and last of their assailants. For this act of bravery and later victories Doodin was made a Hero of the Soviet Union in October 1941. Four other pilots in this regiment were also similarly decorated after gaining ten or more victories.

Over a two-month period the 29th 'Red Banner' IAP claimed 47 enemy aircraft and mounted many ground attacks. For this and the heroism of its pilots the regiment was retitled 1st Guards Fighter Regiment (GvIAP – *Gvardeyskiy istrebitel'nyy aviatsionnyy polk*); it was the first occasion on which an Air Force unit had received this battle honour.

Moscow's first air raid took place on the night of 21st July 1941 and by August, German air attacks on Moscow had intensified. The 6th PVO (*Protivovozdooshnaya oborona*, Air Defence Force) Fighter Corps had been formed on 20th June and charged with Moscow's defence. It was equipped with 783 interceptors, of which 94 were Chaikas but by the end of December only eleven of these remained operational. Many of the losses were attributable to the type being used in the ground attack role. It was a similar situation in

Above: A Red Army Air Force I-153 destroyed on the ground in the first days of the German invasion.

Above: German soldiers examine an apparently undamaged Chaika captured at one of the borderside airfields. The aircraft is equipped with RO-82 launch rails.

The Germans took several flyable I-153s to the Luftwaffe's flight test centre at Rechlin for evaluation. This one came to grief during a test flight.

the defence of Leningrad which was guarded by 242 fighters; of the 38 I-153s in operation in July 1941 only five remained by the end of the year.

Leningrad also enjoyed the support of other I-153s from the Baltic Fleet and also of the VVS, a completely separate organisation from the PVO. On 19th August 1941 air reconnaissance reported that a strong German armoured column was attempting to complete the encirclement of the city and the 7th IAP was ordered by Marshal Kliment Ye. Voroshilov, now commanding the city defences on Stalin's insistence, to destroy the column. Eight I-153 fighters, now in ground attack mode, first halted the column and then broke it up but the leader, Lieutenant (senior grade) N. Svetenko, was forced to land his damaged aircraft in a shell-cratered field behind enemy lines. It was at this point that an almost unbelievable act of bravery took place, worthy of a scene in a James Bond film. Svetenko's second-in-command, A. Slonov, effected a landing between craters, in spite of being under heavy mortar and shell fire, and took off again with Svetenko clutching a wing strut; miraculously, they landed safely at a nearby naval airfield.

I-153s of the PVO, in defence of Moscow, Leningrad and other cities, suffered heavy losses in the first six months of the war and by the end of 1941 only 54 had survived.

Use of the I-153 in various secondary roles continued well into 1943 and it was in that year that another act of almost suicidal heroism was exhibited. Ramming an enemy aircraft is, in itself, a formidable act but A. Sevast'yanov of the 26th IAP not only rammed his quarry, he did it at night. On 6th November he rammed a Heinkel He 111 over Leningrad after exhausting all his ammunition. Debris from both aircraft fell on the garden of the Tauride Palace but the Soviet pilot managed to escape by parachute.

An example of the successful use of RS-82 rockets against aeroplanes took place during an attack on Kronstadt naval base. Regimental Commissar Serbin, in a night attack on an He 111 at 1,000 m (3,280 ft), destroyed it with a rocket salvo. On the way back to base he saw an identical bomber caught in a searchlight beam and shot that one down, too. Altogether this pilot destroyed three He 111s and claimed a share in a fourth.

In the Caucasus the 8th PVO Fighter Corps defending Baku had 266 interceptors, of which 141 were I-153s, but the German offensive towards this area in August 1942 rapidly reduced this number until by the end of November only 20 of the biplanes were left undamaged. This area was considered important enough to be second only to

Moscow in the number of PVO aircraft with which it was defended. As well as being an important oil centre, Baku housed many evacuated defence factories and was a vital entrepôt for supplies from the USA and Britain.

In mid-1943 the VVS had only 36 I-153 and most of the others in service in the west were with the Black Sea Fleet. Some were on the inventories of the 3rd, 4th and 10th GvIAPs, as well as the 7th Detached Flight, PVO. At this time the ten I-153s on Lavensaari Island were having to face the formidable Focke Wulf Fw 190 and a switch was made to a more worthy adversary, the Yak-1 from the 3rd GvIAP.

By 1944 very few of the 3,437 I-153s that had been built were left and the scattered survivors served in second-line duties amongst more modern aircraft. A Luftwaffe intelligence report of February 1944 suggested that only two regiments with whom they had come into conflict at that time had had any Chaikas. In 1945 a few could still be found serving with the Northern Fleet and several more in the Far East, well away from more potent enemies.

The I-153 was not the last type of biplane fighter to enter service in Europe; that dubious honour falls to the Fiat C.R.42 which joined the Regia Aeronautica a few weeks after the I-153 joined the Soviet Air Force. Notwithstanding the fact that the I-153 was considered by most people to be the finest biplane fighter ever designed, it is a great pity that it ever went into production at all. More monoplane fighters would have better served the Soviet Union. However, we all have the benefit of hindsight.

I-153 survivors

Special mention must be made of the three flying examples of the I-153 professionally rebuilt from wrecks by NAPO (former *zavod* 153) in 1996-98 for Sir Tim Wallis of the New Zealand Alpine Fighter Collection. These are

effectively new aircraft with ASh-62IR engines, pneumatically operated undercarriage, radios and GPS receivers. Currently the maximum speed allowed is 385 km/h (239 mph). The Texas-based aircraft is for sale at an asking price of $425,000 plus any taxes.

(In an aside, one can only marvel how the French model kit manufacturer Heller managed to produce an inaccurate model of the I-153, despite having the only surviving genuine example in the world available for close inspection and measurement.)

I-153B project

An attempt to improve the I-153's aerodynamics and reduce maintenance costs was made by eliminating the wing bracing wires. This measure necessitated strengthening and stiffening the wing box by giving the lower wings more taper and also increasing the chord at the roots. It was decided, however, that the advantages were not great enough to justify the disruption of production.

I-153P

I-153P (**push**echnyy – cannon-armed) was the designation given to I-153 fighters armed with two ShVAK 20-mm (.78 calibre) cannons. At the beginning of 1940 three aircraft (c/ns 6578, 6598 and 6760) were each given two synchronised ShVAK cannons and sent to the 16th IAP/24th AD (*aviatsi**on**naya **div**eeziya* – Air Division) of the Moscow Military District for testing under service conditions. Two problems emerged: the extra weight adversely affected manoeuvrability and gunpowder settled on the windscreen during firing, seriously reducing visibility. A further five I-153Ps were produced by *zavod* 1, indicating that a solution had been found for the gunpowder problem. Sources reported that some I-153Ps had their cannons supplemented by two 7.62-mm ShKAS machine-guns but no details or confirmation have been found.

Type	Markings (c/n)	Location	Notes
I-153 M-62	Soviet AF / '9 Red'	*Musée de l'Air et de l'Espace*, Paris	Genuine
I-153	Soviet AF / '10'	Museum of the Northern Fleet Air Arm, Safonovo, near Murmansk	Replica
I-153	Soviet AF / '42 White'	Sukhoi OKB, Moscow	Replica
I-153 ASh-62IR	Soviet AF / '10 Red', registered ZK-JJB	Alpine Fighter Collection, Lake Wanaka, New Zealand	Rebuilt from a 435th IAP aircraft found in Northern Karelia
I-153 ASh-62IR	Soviet AF / '75 White' (7027), registered ZK-JKM	Alpine Fighter Collection, Lake Wanaka, New Zealand	Rebuilt from an 826th IAP aircraft found in Northern Karelia
I-153 ASh-62IR	Soviet AF / '16 Red' (6316), registered ZK-JKN	Lone Star Flight Museum, Galveston, Texas	Rebuilt from a 2nd IAP, Northern Fleet Air Arm aircraft found near Murmansk

Above: The sole I-153UD prototype. The wooden monocoque rear fuselage is clearly visible, revealed by the smooth plywood skin without the stringers characteristically showing through the fabric rear fuselage skin of the standard Chaika.

This I-153 was powered by a turbocharged M-62 engine; note the shiny supercharger fairing.

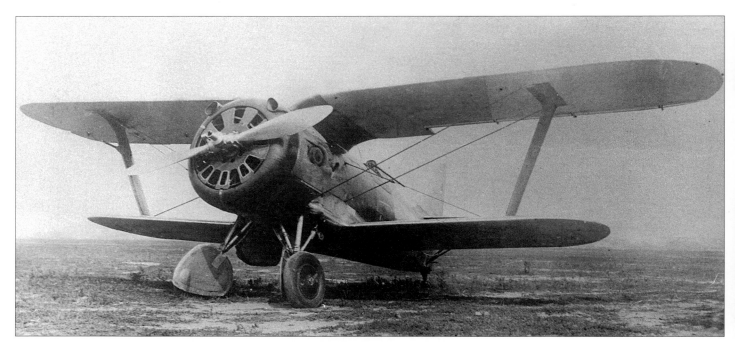

Above: One of the I-153TK development aircraft, showing the characteristic twin air intakes, one for each supercharger.

Left: Another I-153TK with a different cowling design incorporating an oil cooler at the bottom. The superchargers are exposed to a greater extent.

Below left: The M-63 engine of the same aircraft, showing the exhaust manifold and air duct connected to the port TK-1 supercharger.

I-153Sh ground attack aircraft

This designation (Sh = *shtoormovik*, ground attack aircraft) was used in 1940 for the prototype of a ground attack version of the I-153 which carried under its lower wings up to four teardrop-shaped containers, each of which contained a 7.62-mm ShKAS machine-gun.

I-153USh ground attack aircraft

Another ground attack prototype that was tried in 1940 was equipped with two cylindrical containers under its lower wings. Each held 20 2.5-kg (5.5-lb) bomblets or chemical weapons

I-153TK high-altitude fighter

As previously mentioned, the Soviet High Command were concerned about the German development of high-altitude reconnaissance bombers (Junkers Ju 86P) so, in response, between 19th July and 29th August 1939, four I-153s (construction numbers 6001, 6003, 6006 and 6011) were used for testing M-25V and M-62 engines, each with two TK-1 turbo-superchargers. These aircraft were known as the I-153TK (*s toorbokompressorom*, with turbo-supercharger). With the M-25V, top speed was 455 km/h (283 mph) at 8,750 m (28,700 ft) and with the M-62, 482 km/h (300 mph) at 10,300 m (33,800 ft). However, with the

Above: I-153 c/n 6024 with DM-4 ramjet boosters. These were carried on the standard bomb racks.

Right: The same aircraft with the earlier DM-2 boosters, September 1940. Note how much larger the later model is.

Below right: The canopy of the I-153GK.

TK-1 inoperative the aircraft were slower and less manoeuvrable at all altitudes as a result of the increased weight. Although the adverse effects outweighed the benefits for general use, in 1940 a small batch of 20 I-153TKs with M-62s and one with an M-63 engine was built for interception at high altitudes.

I-153UD (I-153U.D.) development aircraft

A concern about the availability of metals was the motivation in building this prototype with a wooden rear fuselage. The aircraft was known as the I-153UD or I-153U.D. (probably standing for *oosover**shen**stvovannyy, dere-**vian**nyy* – improved, wooden). A frame with longerons and stringers was covered in shpon, a form of plywood manufactured from strips of birch wood bonded together with casein glue each layer being at right angles to the next to provide extra strength. A similar structure was used on the I-16. This monocoque rear fuselage weighed 8.4 kg (18.5 lb) more than the standard unit and the contours were identical. A prototype was built and tested from 30th September to 5th October 1940 and although it performed satisfactorily, the project was discontinued, as production of the I-153 was to cease at the end of the year.

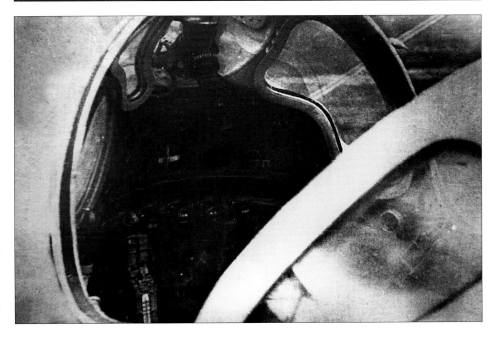

Above: The I-153GK (c/n 6028) at GK NII VVS during State Acceptance Trials. Note how the cockpit canopy slides inside the fuselage when opened.

Above: Another view of the I-153GK at GK NII VVS with the canopy closed.

Three-quarters front view of the I-153GK with the canopy open. A large spinner appears to have been fitted originally, judging by the darker coloured circle around the small spinner.

I-153V or I-153GK high-altitude fighter

The I-153V (*vysotnyy*, high-altitude), alias I-153GK (*s ghermeticheskoy kabinoy*, with pressure cabin), was an I-153 M-63 (construction number 6028) fitted with the latest pressure cabin developed by Aleksandr Ya. Schcherbakov. The cabin was made from welded aluminium alloy and fitted with rubber seals over all apertures. A final airtight seal was achieved by clamping the hood to the rubber moulding around the sides of the cockpit's 6 mm (0.23 in.) thick Plexiglas. The heavily framed hinged hood gave vastly improved pilot vision compared to previous models which had only porthole-like apertures in a metal cupola. Once again the trials in June and July 1940 were technically successful but the overall weight increase of 190 kg (420 lb) degraded performance, rendering the project unviable.

I-153V-TKGK high-altitude fighter

This was an M-63 engined version of the I-153 fitted in late 1939 with twin TK-3 turbochargers and a lighter and more flexible Shcherbakov pressure cabin; the long suffix to the designation stood for *vysotnyy, s toorbokompressorami i ghermeticheskoy kabinoy* (high-altitude, with turbosuperchargers and pressure cabin). Trials had just begun when the newly formed NKAP (*Narodnyy komissariaht aviatsionnoy promyshlennosti*, People's Commissariat for the Aviation Industry) ordered them to be stopped.

I-153 M-65

The designation I-153 M-65 indicated an I-153 prototype with an M-65 engine which was tested in 1940. No details are known of the engine or of the tests.

I-153DM (I-153PVRD)

The I-153DM (*dopolnitel'nyye motory*, supplementary motors) or I-153PVRD (*pryamotochnyye vozdooshno-reaktivnyye dvigateli*, ramjets) was an I-153 (construction number 6024) which in September 1940 was fitted with two Merkoolov DM-2 ramjet boosters of 400 mm (15.75 in.) diameter installed under the lower wings on the standard hardpoints. These supplementary engines were 1,500 mm (59 in.) long and weighed only 19 kg (62 lb), including mountings. A 30 km/h (19 mph) increase in top speed when the ramjets were started was recorded by test pilots P. Ye. Loginov, A. V. Davydov and A. I. Zhookov. Trials were carried out in October of the same year with 500 mm (19.7 in) diameter DM-4 engines when a maximum speed increase of 51 km/h (32 mph) was achieved. In total, 74 test flights were completed with both types of ramjet.

Chapter 6

The Last of the Kind

I-170 project (*izdeliye* M)

The I-170 was a projected but never built I-153 variant with a wooden fuselage, tapered wings having an area of 25 sq. m (269 sq. ft), and a liquid-cooled M-106 engine. A top speed of 500 km/h (311 mph) was anticipated when work on it commenced in the late summer of 1939 under the designation *izdeliye* M. Installation of the M-64 radial engine and the liquid-cooled 12-cylinder M-105 (the latter designed by Vladimir Ya. Klimov) was also considered. Design work on the M-106 version was expected to be completed by 15th October 1939 and a mock-up ready four weeks later. In October Polikarpov departed to Germany and on his return found he had lost 80 of his staff to the new Mikoyan team and that all work on the I-170 had ceased.

I-190 experimental fighter

The I-190 was developed at *zavod* 156 over a two-year period from the end of January 1938 as the successor to the I-153. It was to be powered by the M-88 engine designed by

Sergey K. Tumanskiy and driving an AV-2L variable pitch propeller. To ease the factory's switch from I-153 production, a great effort was made for the two models to have as many parts in common as possible. Nevertheless, major improvements were made: the wings had plywood skins, the horizontal tail was cantilevered, the tailwheel made retractable, a larger vertical tail was fitted and the armament of production aircraft was to be two ShVAK 20-mm cannons or four ShKAS 7.62-mm machine-guns plus up to 200 kg (442 lb) of bombs.

A mock-up was produced in the autumn of 1938, then Polikarpov's OKB moved to *zavod* 1 in February 1939 and the first flight of the I-190, now on skis, took place on 30th December 1939 with A. I. Zhookov as pilot. The engine was a direct drive version, the M-88BRL (BR = *bezredooktornyy* – with no reduction gearbox), with a three-blade propeller. Problems with the uneven running of the engine plagued flight tests and culminat-

ed in an emergency landing, fortunately successful, after the seventh flight. In April 1940 testing was suspended when the aircraft was involved in an accident but resumed two weeks later on completion of repairs. During mid-April 1940 an M-88R geared engine (R = *redooktornyy*) was installed together with a modified cowling, but constant overheating proved a serious problem. Yet another engine switch, this time to an M-88A, gave only a few more flights before the trials were terminated after the aircraft was damaged in a forced landing at Tushino on 13th February 1941. A disappointing maximum speed of 488 km/h (303 mph) at 5,000 m (16,400 ft) had been recorded in these tests.

In the meantime, at *zavod* 1, a second prototype I-190 was being built, this time powered by an M-88 equipped with a TK-1 turbocharger. Work had also just started on a variant with two TK-1s and a pressurised cockpit but the NKAP ordered that all development on the I-190 be stopped before the

The I-190 prototype powered by an M-88BRL taking shape at the Moscow aircraft factory No. 39.

Above: The I-190 on skis during manufacturer's flight tests. The aircraft was painted light grey overall.

Head-on view of the I-190.

Above: A side view of the I-190 prototype. The ink stamp reads *Sekretno* **(classified).**

Rear view of the I-190.

The I-190 programme was terminated after this crash landing on 13th February 1941 in which the first prototype was written off. Note the forward-retracting tailwheel; also note that the engine cowling has been repainted a darker colour.

plane was to have the much more powerful 1,500-hp (1,119-kW) M-90 engine, with a ducted spinner supplying the cooling air. Other known details are: length 7.65 m (25.1 ft), wing area 28.0 sq. m (301 sq. ft), loaded weight to be 2,916 kg (6,429 lb) and an estimated maximum speed of 590 km/h (367 mph) at about 7,000 m (23,000 ft) reducing to 510 km/h (317 mph) at sea level. Intended armament was two 20 mm ShVAK cannons and two 12.7 mm machine-guns and up to 250 kg (550 lb) of bombs.

This was the final attempt by Polikarpov to design a biplane fighter. He abandoned the work after metaphorically shooting himself down in flames by producing a paper attesting that vertical, not horizontal, manoeuvrability was the more important parameter in determining the victor of an aerial combat. It was very surprising to find him still designing biplane fighters in 1940 and one wonders if the outcome would have been different if he had focused the work of the OKB on the I-180 and later the I-185 instead of accepting the additional burden of all these biplanes.

Data for the I-190 with M-88 engine:

Span:	
upper wings	10.2 m (33.5 ft)
lower wings	7.5 m (24.6 ft)
Length	6.5 m (21.3 ft)
Wing area	24.83 m² (267 sq. ft)
Weight:	
empty	1,761 kg (3,882 lb)
loaded	2,112 kg (4,656 lb)
Fuel weight	200 kg (442 lb)
Oil weight	20 kg (44 lb)
Maximum speed:	
at sea level	375 km/h (233 mph)
at 5,000 m (16,400 ft)	488 km/h (303 mph)
at 7,050 m (23,130 ft)	450 km/h (279 mph)
Climb to 5,000 m	5.9 minutes
Service ceiling	12,400 m (40,700 ft)
Range	720 km (447 miles)

second prototype was finished. It would be reassuring to believe that this decision was occasioned by the realisation that biplanes were outmoded, but a more likely explanation is to be found in the report delivered by Yakov V. Smooshkevich, head of the VVS, to the Communist Party Central Committee on 14th May 1940 declaring that M-63, M-88 and M-105 engines were so unreliable as to have become an obstacle to the development of new aircraft. It is ironic that each one later became a successful engine.

It is impossible not to feel pity for Polikarpov at this stage because the performance of the M-88 was also threatening his trials of the I-180, the intended replacement for his monoplane fighter, the I-16.

Only two prototypes of the I-190 were built, one of which was not completed.

I-195 project

The I-195 project of 1940 was for a strengthened version of the I-190 with an enclosed but unpressurised cockpit. This unbraced sesqui-

It is a measure of Polikarpov's greatness that, up to 1940, more were built of his aircraft of all types and functions than those of all other Soviet designers put together. Admittedly this feat was mainly achieved because he was responsible for the development of the U-2, later renamed Polikarpov Po-2, a trainer and general-purpose biplane prolifically produced over a long period of time. About 33,000 have been built in the Soviet Union, Yugoslavia and Poland, and home-built examples are still appearing. However, he had also been responsible for the I-5, I-15, I-15*bis*, I-153 and I-16 which formed over 90% of the fighter inventory of the PVO, the Soviet Air Force and Naval Air Arm in 1939. He was in his time truly 'the King of Fighters'.

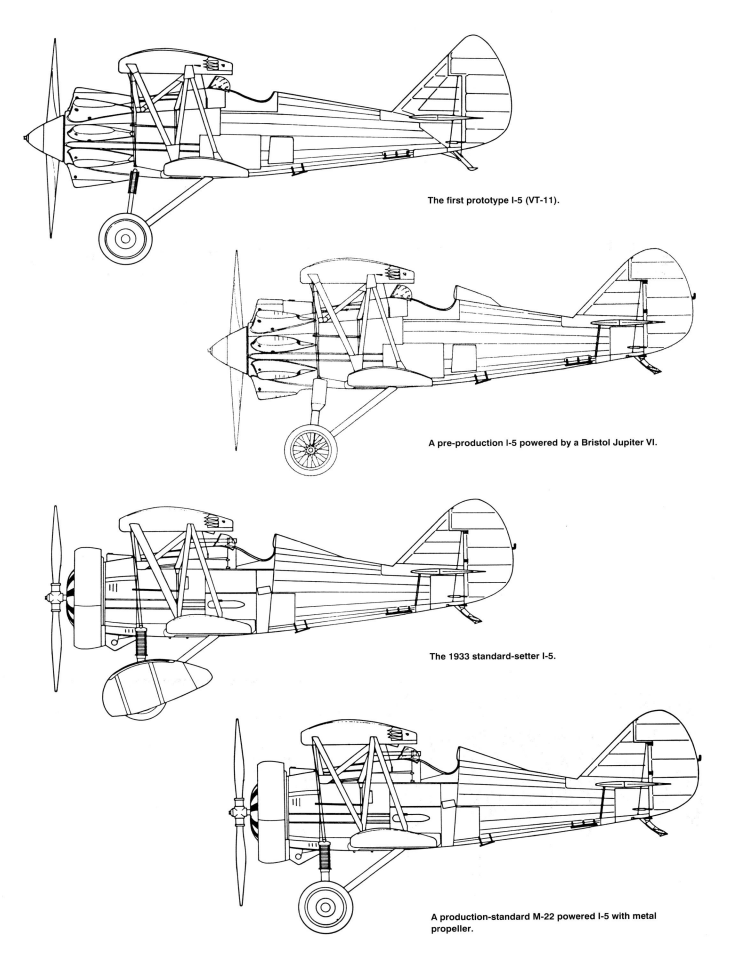

The first prototype I-5 (VT-11).

A pre-production I-5 powered by a Bristol Jupiter VI.

The 1933 standard-setter I-5.

A production-standard M-22 powered I-5 with metal propeller.

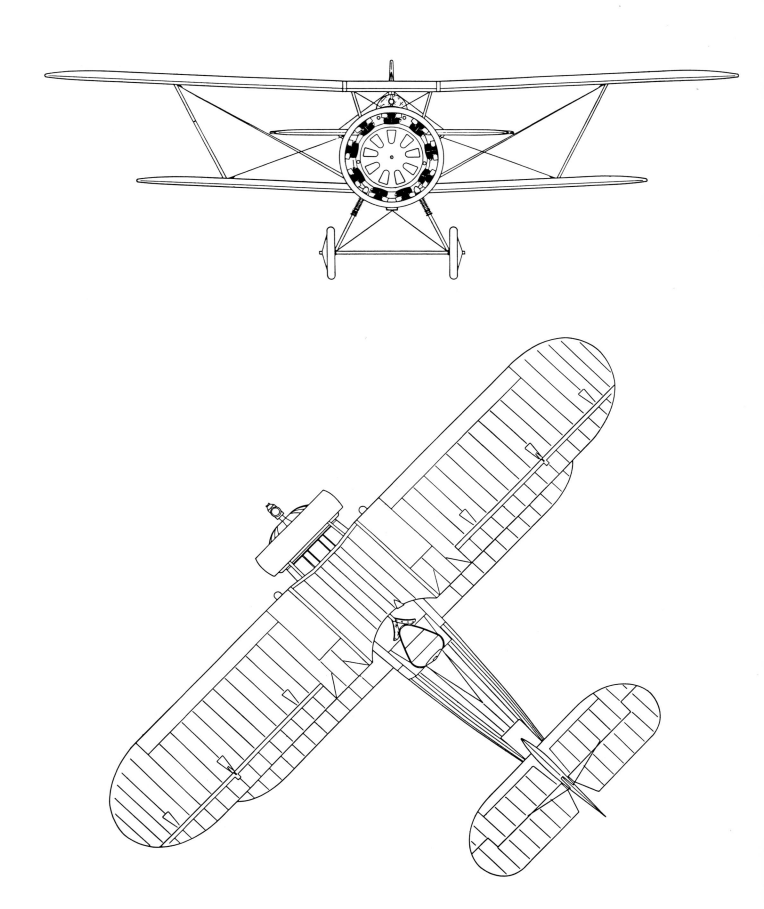

Front and upper views of a typical I-5 M-22; the propeller hub is not shown in the front view.

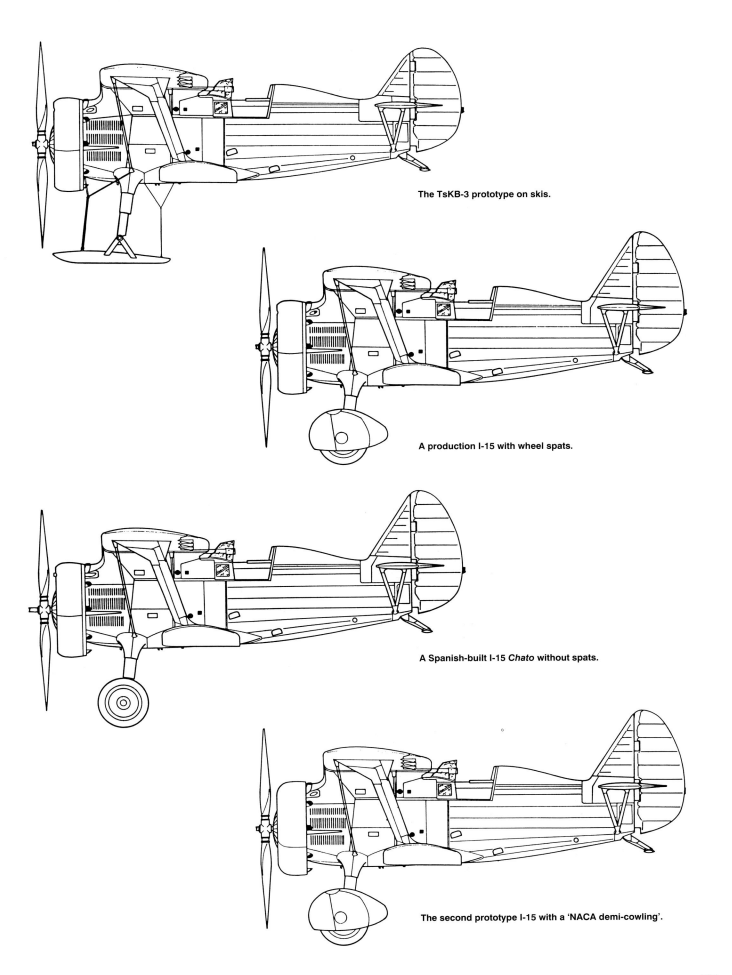

The TsKB-3 prototype on skis.

A production I-15 with wheel spats.

A Spanish-built I-15 *Chato* without spats.

The second prototype I-15 with a 'NACA demi-cowling'.

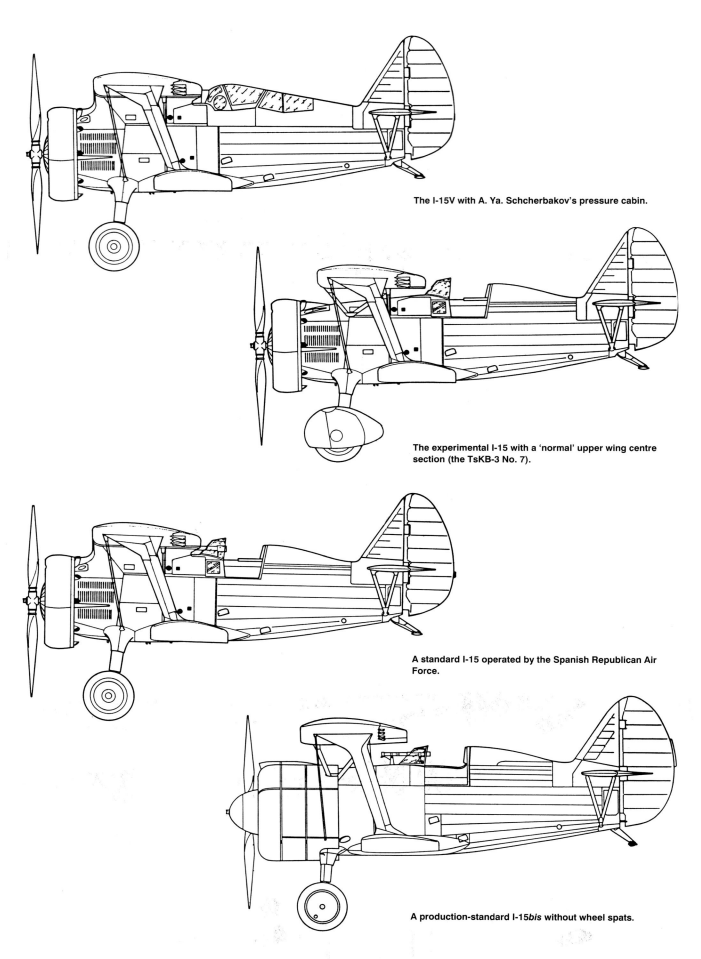

The I-15V with A. Ya. Schcherbakov's pressure cabin.

The experimental I-15 with a 'normal' upper wing centre section (the TsKB-3 No. 7).

A standard I-15 operated by the Spanish Republican Air Force.

A production-standard I-15*bis* without wheel spats.

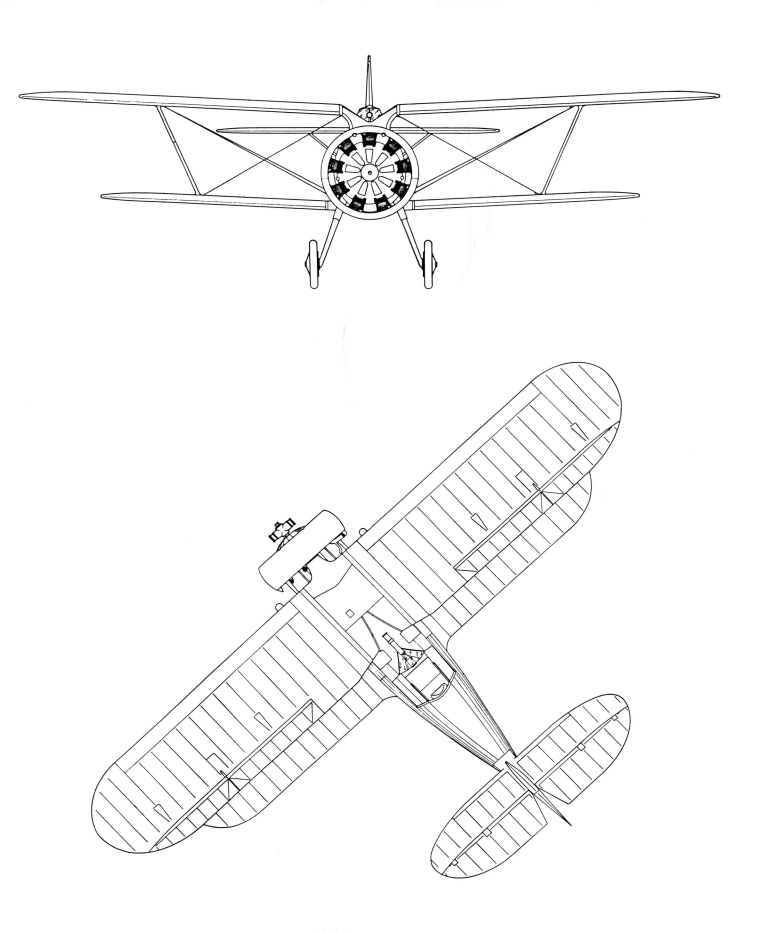

Front and upper views of the I-15.

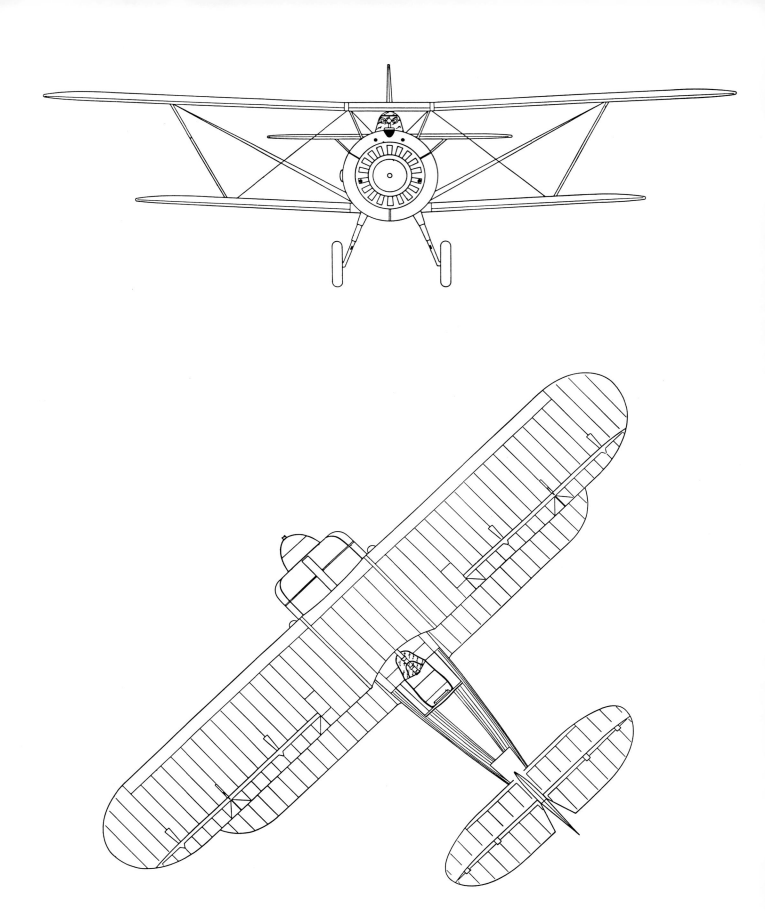

Front and upper views of the I-15*bis*.

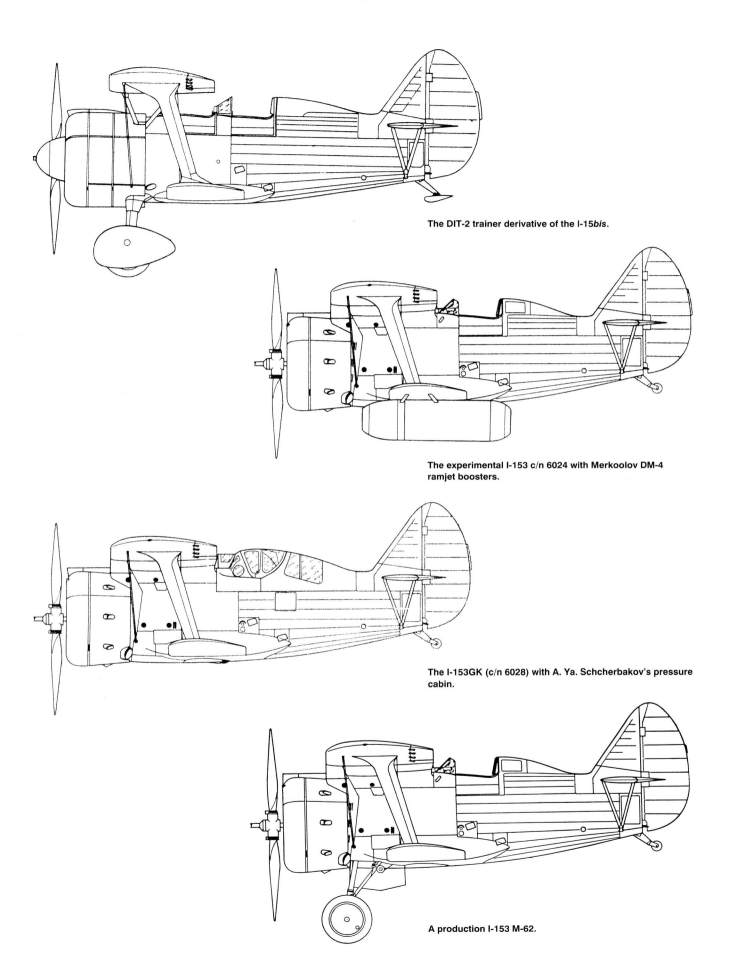

The DIT-2 trainer derivative of the I-15*bis*.

The experimental I-153 c/n 6024 with Merkoolov DM-4 ramjet boosters.

The I-153GK (c/n 6028) with A. Ya. Schcherbakov's pressure cabin.

A production I-153 M-62.

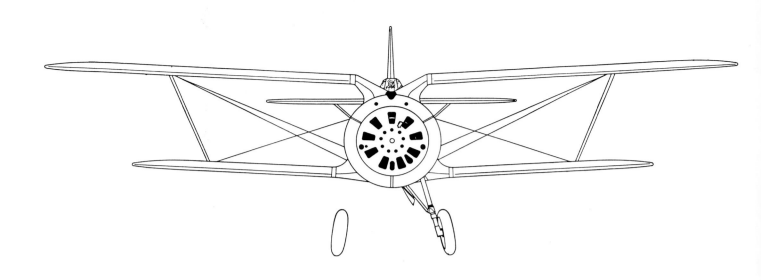

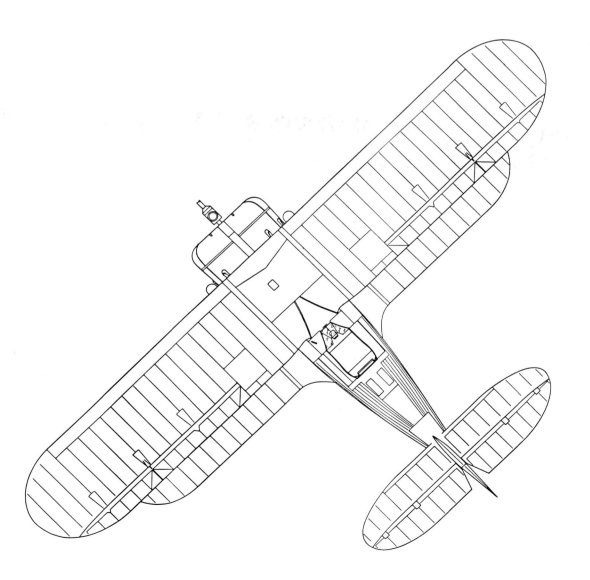

Front and upper views of the I-153 M-62. Note the 'toe-out'
position of the mainwheels in extended position.

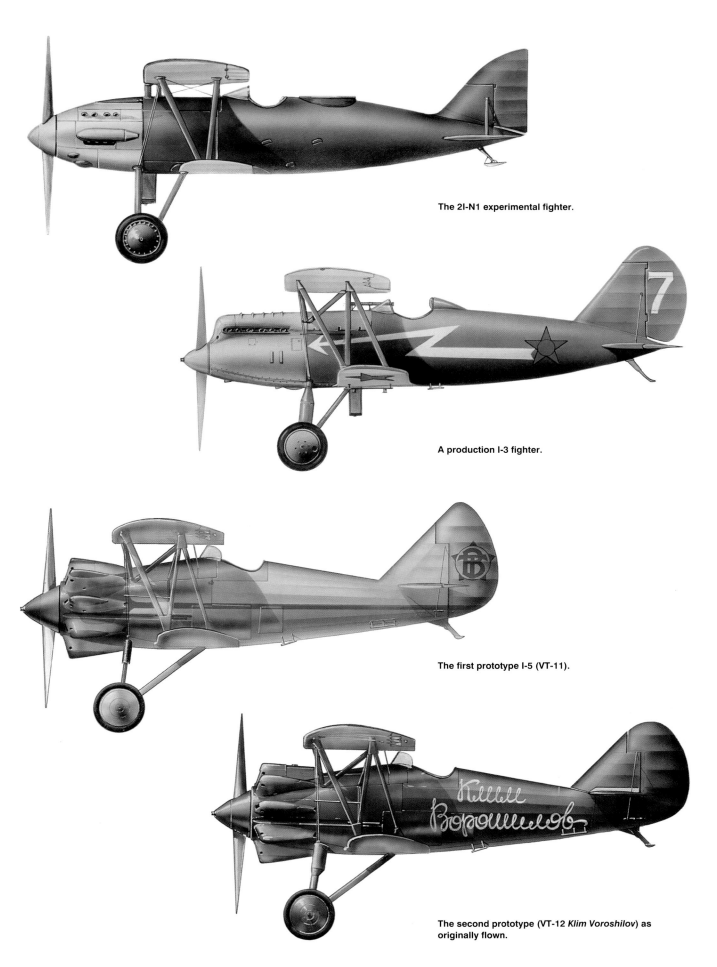

The 2I-N1 experimental fighter.

A production I-3 fighter.

The first prototype I-5 (VT-11).

The second prototype (VT-12 *Klim Voroshilov*) as originally flown.

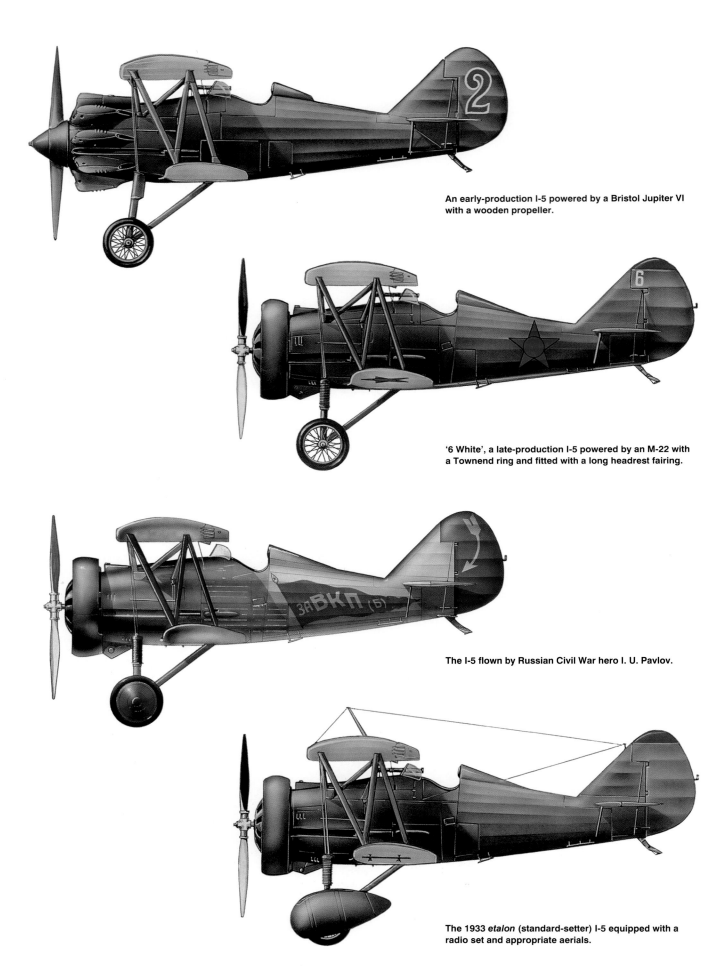

An early-production I-5 powered by a Bristol Jupiter VI with a wooden propeller.

'6 White', a late-production I-5 powered by an M-22 with a Townend ring and fitted with a long headrest fairing.

The I-5 flown by Russian Civil War hero I. U. Pavlov.

The 1933 *etalon* (standard-setter) I-5 equipped with a radio set and appropriate aerials.

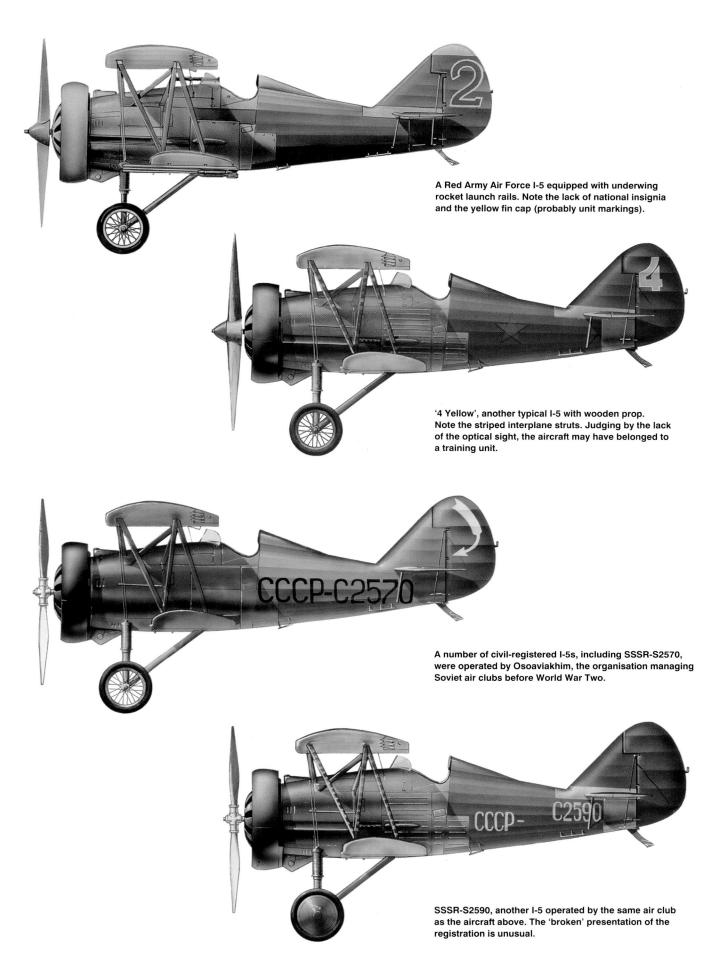

A Red Army Air Force I-5 equipped with underwing rocket launch rails. Note the lack of national insignia and the yellow fin cap (probably unit markings).

'4 Yellow', another typical I-5 with wooden prop. Note the striped interplane struts. Judging by the lack of the optical sight, the aircraft may have belonged to a training unit.

A number of civil-registered I-5s, including SSSR-S2570, were operated by Osoaviakhim, the organisation managing Soviet air clubs before World War Two.

SSSR-S2590, another I-5 operated by the same air club as the aircraft above. The 'broken' presentation of the registration is unusual.

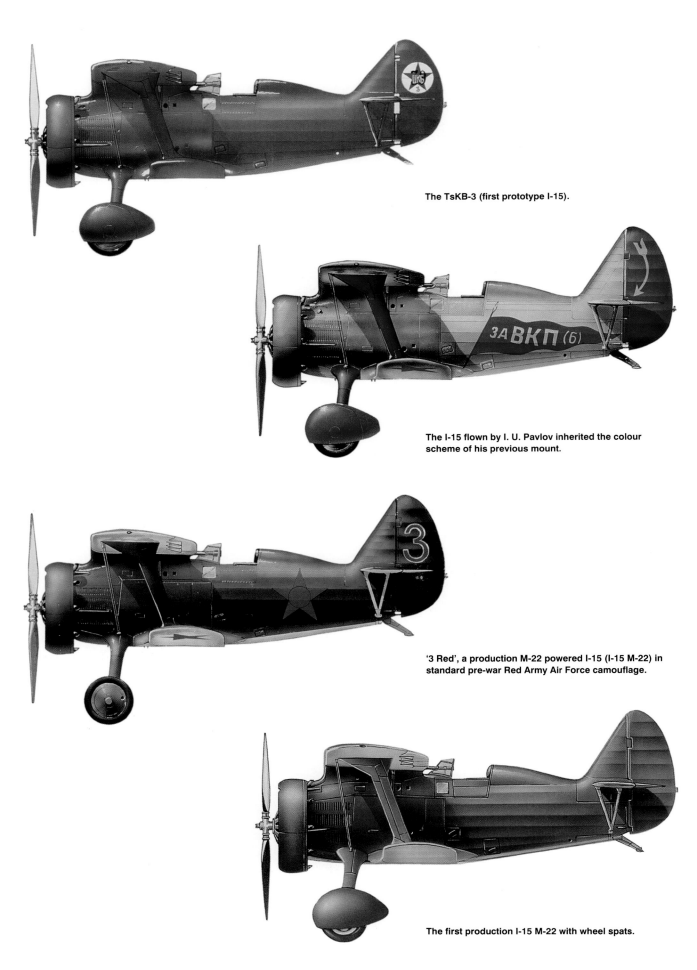

The TsKB-3 (first prototype I-15).

The I-15 flown by I. U. Pavlov inherited the colour scheme of his previous mount.

'3 Red', a production M-22 powered I-15 (I-15 M-22) in standard pre-war Red Army Air Force camouflage.

The first production I-15 M-22 with wheel spats.

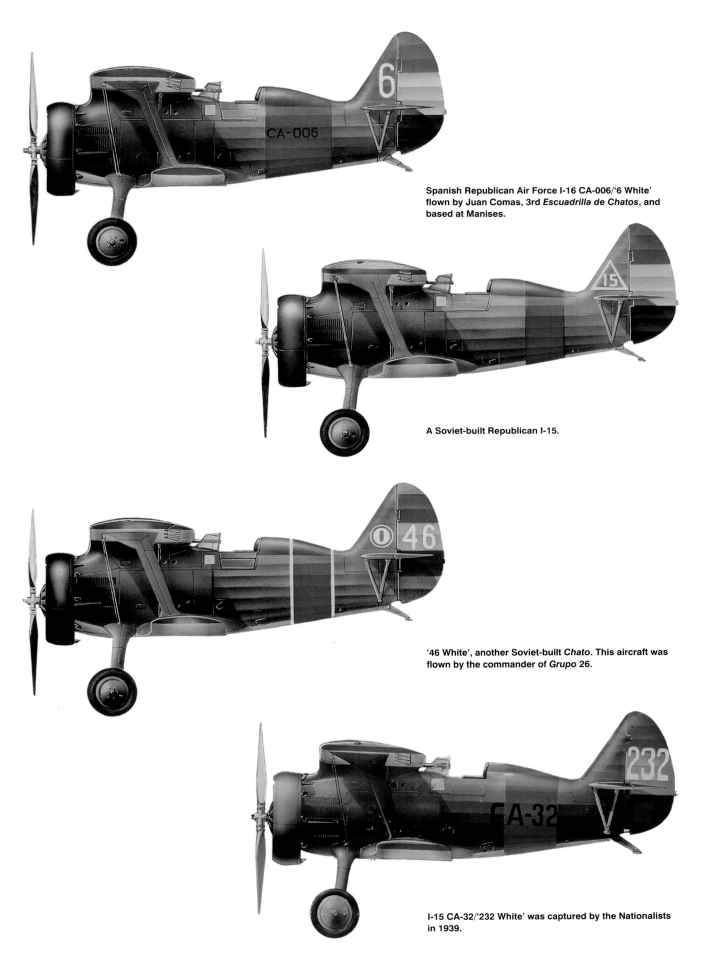

Spanish Republican Air Force I-16 CA-006/'6 White' flown by Juan Comas, 3rd *Escuadrilla de Chatos*, and based at Manises.

A Soviet-built Republican I-15.

'46 White', another Soviet-built *Chato*. This aircraft was flown by the commander of *Grupo* 26.

I-15 CA-32/'232 White' was captured by the Nationalists in 1939.

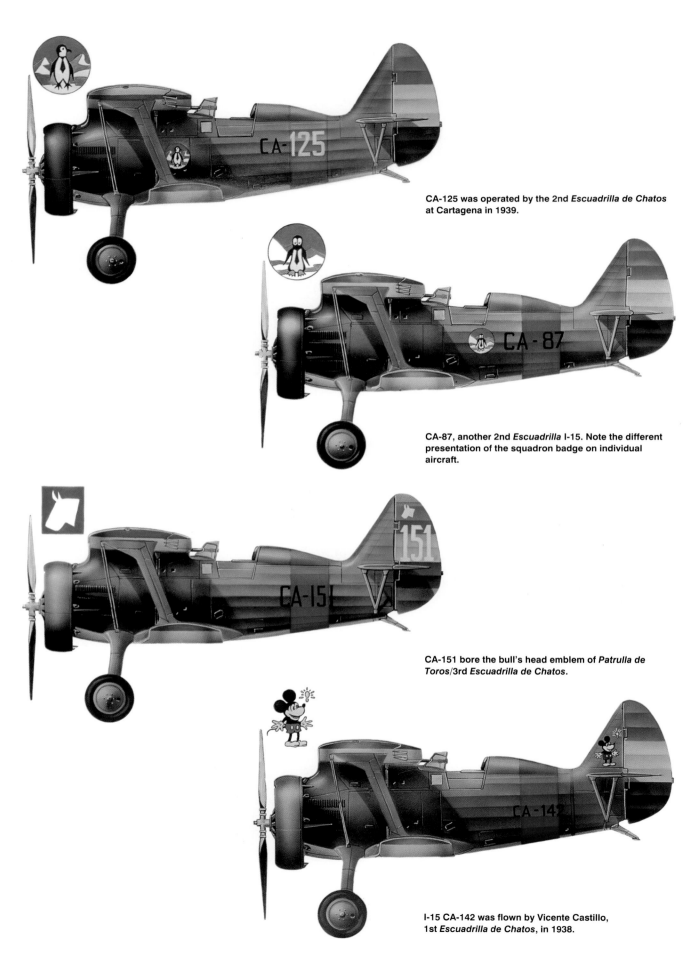

CA-125 was operated by the 2nd *Escuadrilla de Chatos* at Cartagena in 1939.

CA-87, another 2nd *Escuadrilla* I-15. Note the different presentation of the squadron badge on individual aircraft.

CA-151 bore the bull's head emblem of *Patrulla de Toros*/3rd *Escuadrilla de Chatos*.

I-15 CA-142 was flown by Vicente Castillo, 1st *Escuadrilla de Chatos*, in 1938.

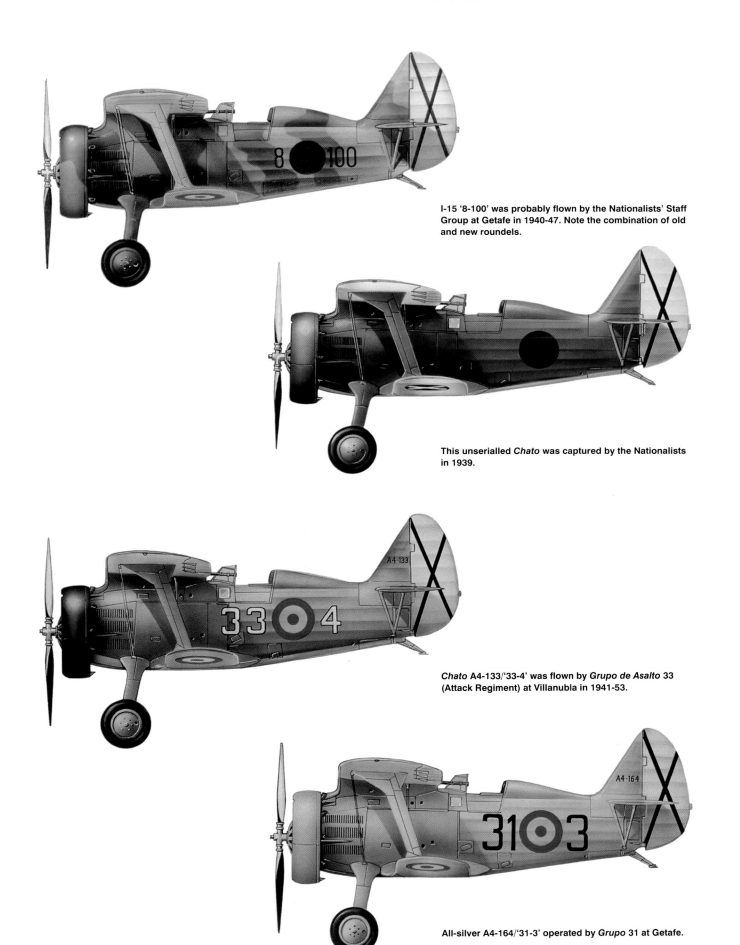

I-15 '8-100' was probably flown by the Nationalists' Staff Group at Getafe in 1940-47. Note the combination of old and new roundels.

This unserialled *Chato* was captured by the Nationalists in 1939.

Chato A4-133/'33-4' was flown by *Grupo de Asalto* 33 (Attack Regiment) at Villanubla in 1941-53.

All-silver A4-164/'31-3' operated by *Grupo* 31 at Getafe.

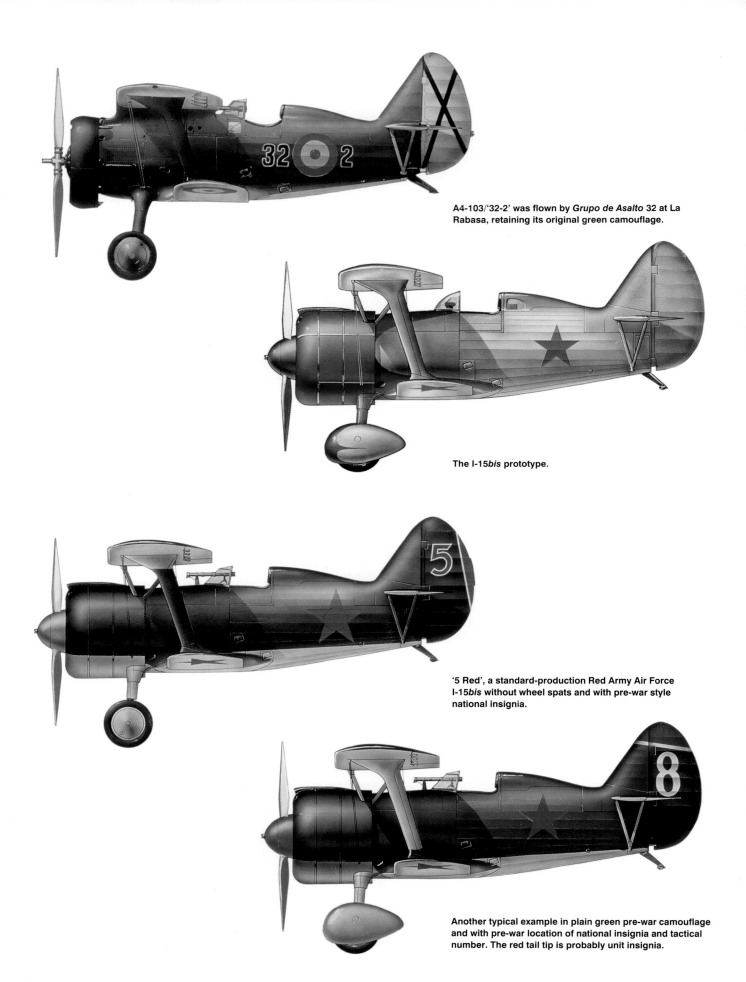

A4-103/'32-2' was flown by *Grupo de Asalto* 32 at La Rabasa, retaining its original green camouflage.

The I-15*bis* prototype.

'5 Red', a standard-production Red Army Air Force I-15*bis* without wheel spats and with pre-war style national insignia.

Another typical example in plain green pre-war camouflage and with pre-war location of national insignia and tactical number. The red tail tip is probably unit insignia.

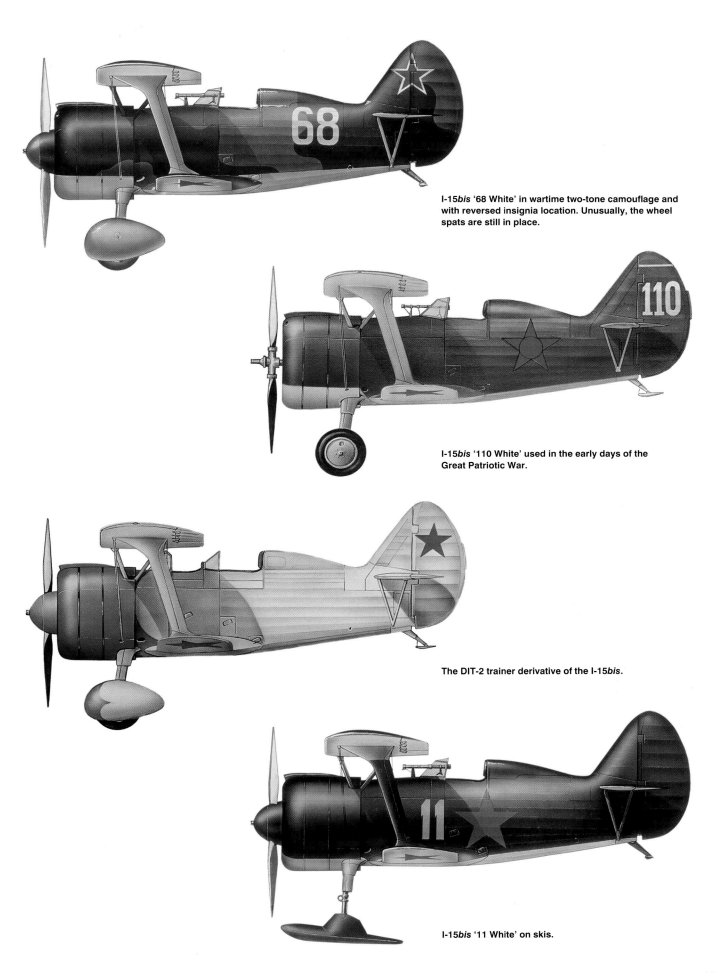

I-15*bis* '68 White' in wartime two-tone camouflage and with reversed insignia location. Unusually, the wheel spats are still in place.

I-15*bis* '110 White' used in the early days of the Great Patriotic War.

The DIT-2 trainer derivative of the I-15*bis*.

I-15*bis* '11 White' on skis.

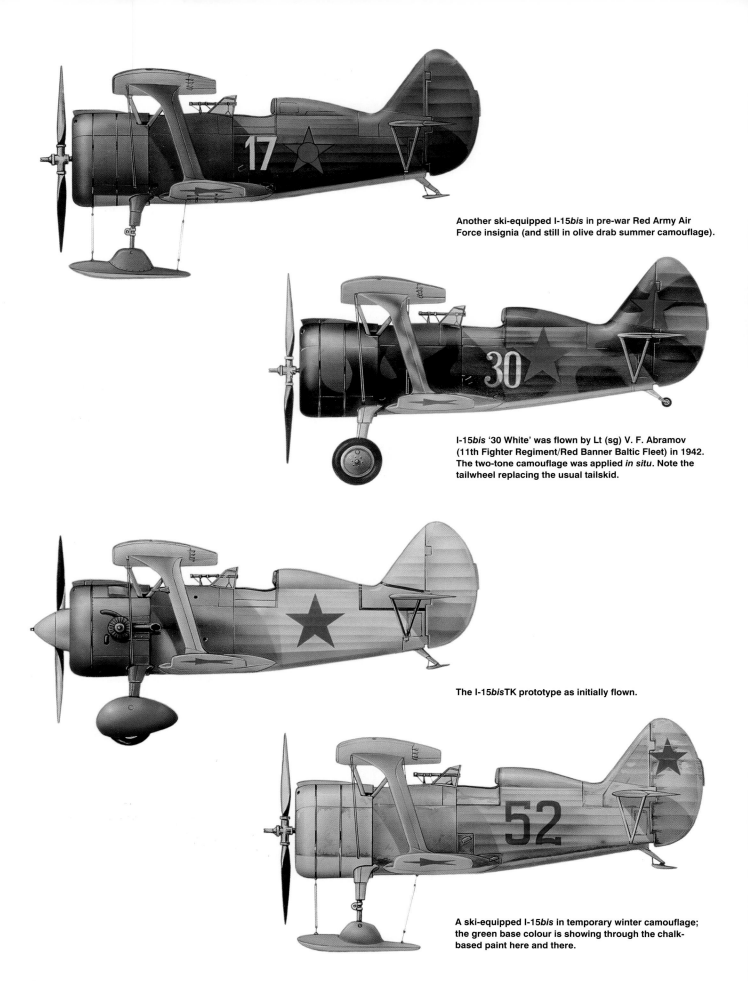

Another ski-equipped I-15*bis* in pre-war Red Army Air Force insignia (and still in olive drab summer camouflage).

I-15*bis* '30 White' was flown by Lt (sg) V. F. Abramov (11th Fighter Regiment/Red Banner Baltic Fleet) in 1942. The two-tone camouflage was applied *in situ*. Note the tailwheel replacing the usual tailskid.

The I-15*bis*TK prototype as initially flown.

A ski-equipped I-15*bis* in temporary winter camouflage; the green base colour is showing through the chalk-based paint here and there.

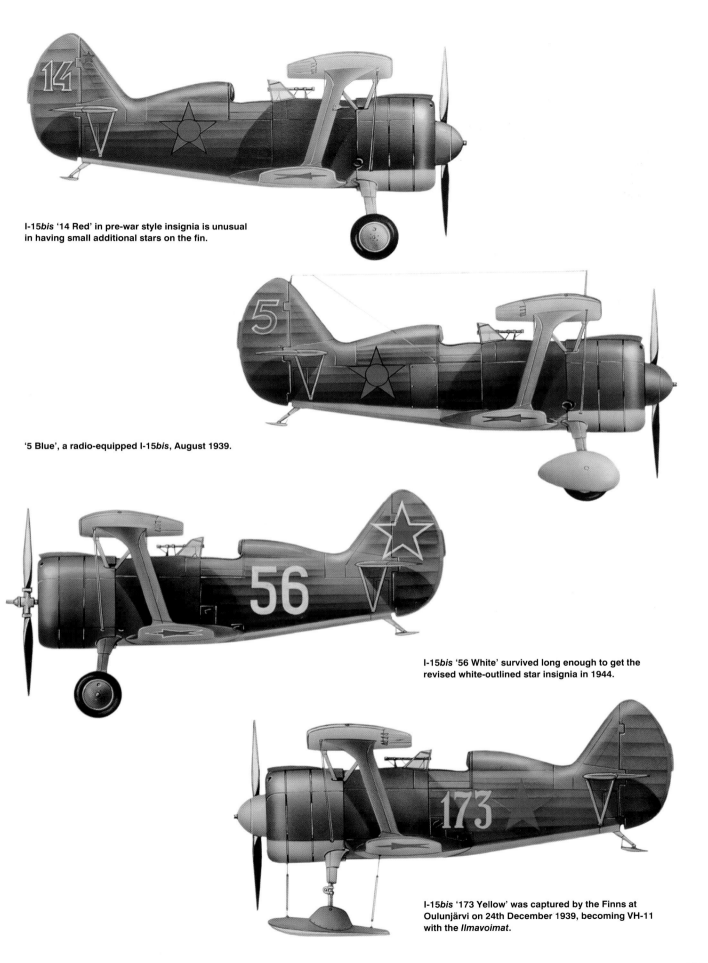

I-15*bis* '14 Red' in pre-war style insignia is unusual in having small additional stars on the fin.

'5 Blue', a radio-equipped I-15*bis*, August 1939.

I-15*bis* '56 White' survived long enough to get the revised white-outlined star insignia in 1944.

I-15*bis* '173 Yellow' was captured by the Finns at Oulunjärvi on 24th December 1939, becoming VH-11 with the *Ilmavoimat*.

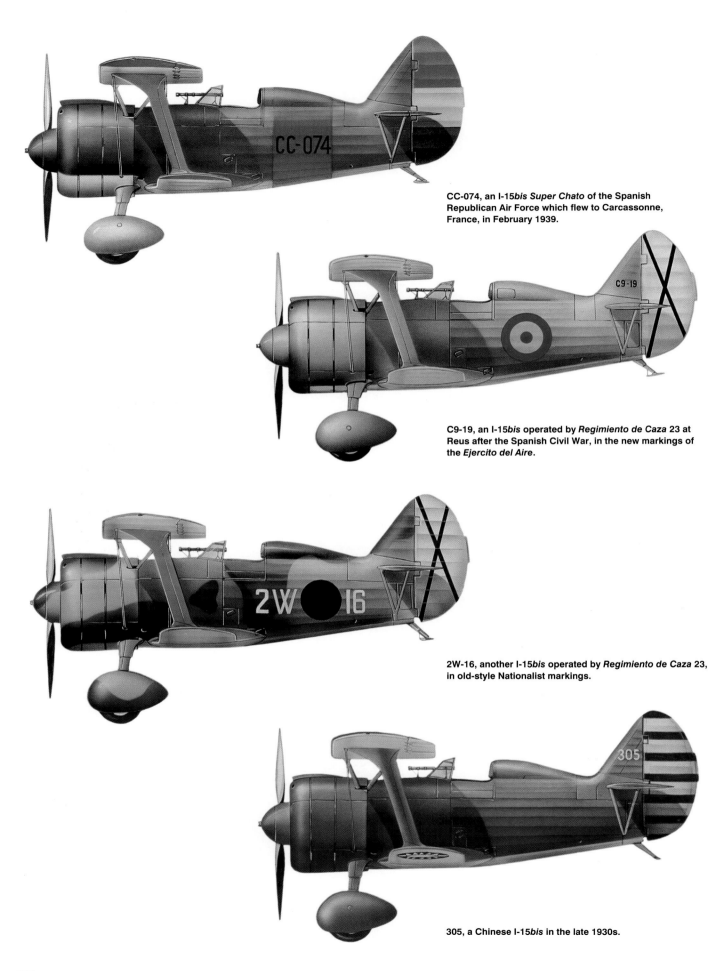

CC-074, an I-15*bis* *Super Chato* of the Spanish Republican Air Force which flew to Carcassonne, France, in February 1939.

C9-19, an I-15*bis* operated by *Regimiento de Caza* 23 at Reus after the Spanish Civil War, in the new markings of the *Ejercito del Aire*.

2W-16, another I-15*bis* operated by *Regimiento de Caza* 23, in old-style Nationalist markings.

305, a Chinese I-15*bis* in the late 1930s.

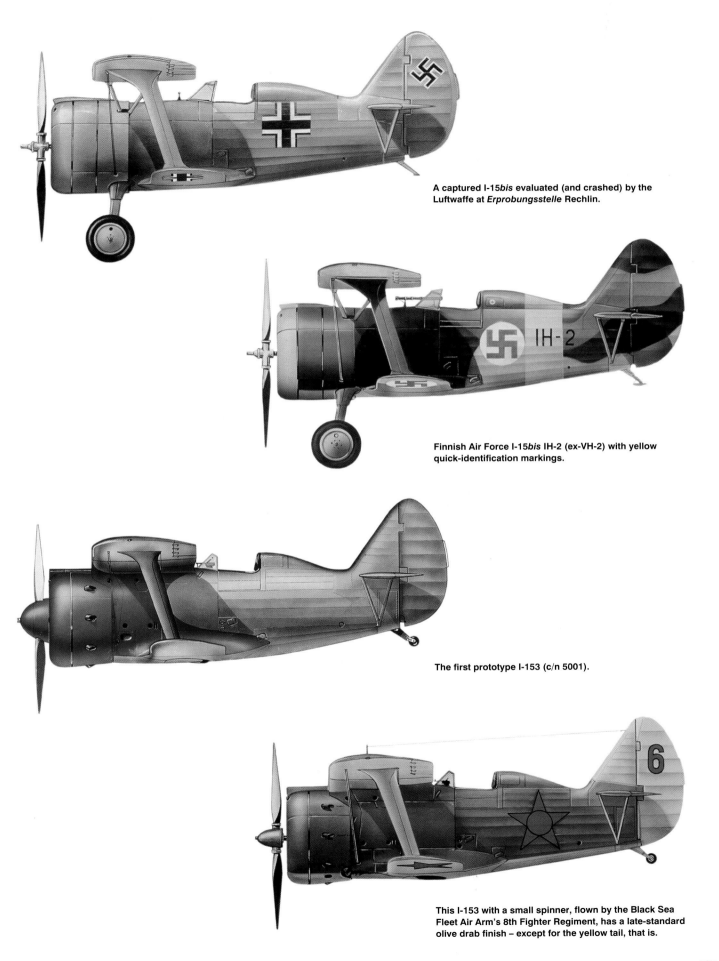

A captured I-15*bis* evaluated (and crashed) by the Luftwaffe at *Erprobungsstelle* Rechlin.

Finnish Air Force I-15*bis* IH-2 (ex-VH-2) with yellow quick-identification markings.

The first prototype I-153 (c/n 5001).

This I-153 with a small spinner, flown by the Black Sea Fleet Air Arm's 8th Fighter Regiment, has a late-standard olive drab finish – except for the yellow tail, that is.

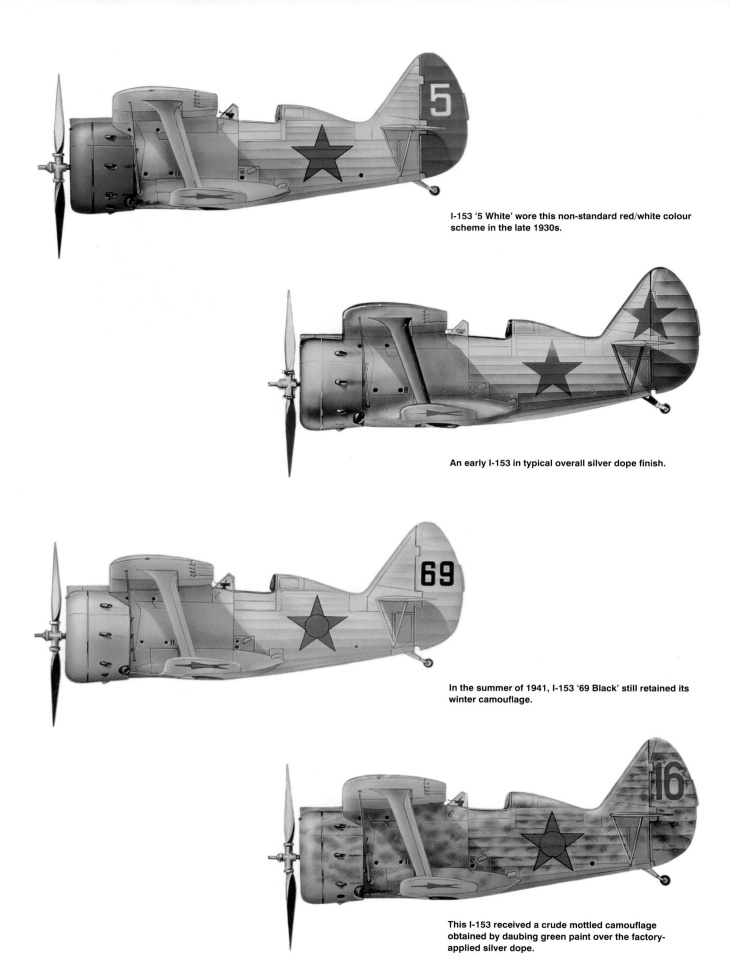

I-153 '5 White' wore this non-standard red/white colour scheme in the late 1930s.

An early I-153 in typical overall silver dope finish.

In the summer of 1941, I-153 '69 Black' still retained its winter camouflage.

This I-153 received a crude mottled camouflage obtained by daubing green paint over the factory-applied silver dope.

A 7th Fighter Regiment I-153 in locally-applied two-tone camouflage, on the Leningrad Front, 1941.

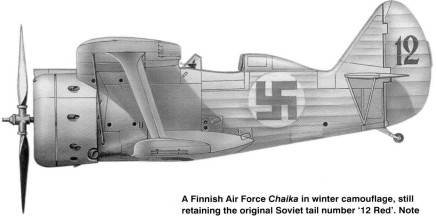

A Finnish Air Force *Chaika* in winter camouflage, still retaining the original Soviet tail number '12 Red'. Note that the quick-identification markings are applied only to the undersides for the benefit of the ground troops.

Another *Ilmavoimat* I-153, this time with the Finnish serial IT-21

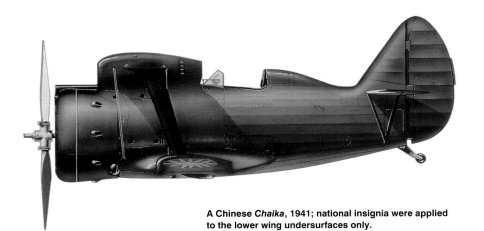

A Chinese *Chaika*, 1941; national insignia were applied to the lower wing undersurfaces only.

Red Star Volume 1
SUKHOI S-37 & MIKOYAN MFI

Yefim Gordon

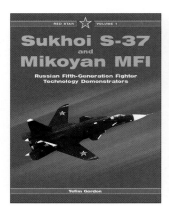

Conceived as an answer to the American ATF programme, the Mikoyan MFI (better known as the 1.42 or 1.44) and the Sukhoi S-37 Berkoot were developed as technology demonstrators. Both design bureaux used an approach that was quite different from Western fifth-generation fighter philosophy. This gives a detailed account of how these enigmatic aircraft were designed, built and flown. It includes structural descriptions of both types.

Sbk, 280 x 215 mm, 96pp, plus 8pp colour foldout, 12 b/w and 174 colour photos, drawings and colour artworks
1 85780 120 2 **£18.95/US $27.95**

Red Star Volume 2
FLANKERS: The New Generation

Yefim Gordon

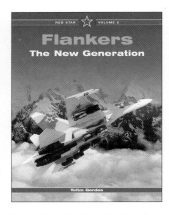

The multi-role Su-30 and Su-35 and thrust-vectoring Su-37 are described in detail, along with the 'big head' Su-23FN/Su-34 tactical bomber, the Su-27K (Su-33) shipborne fighter and its two-seat combat trainer derivative, the Su-27KUB. The book also describes the customised versions developed for foreign customers – the Su-30KI (Su-27KI), the Su-30MKI for India, the Su-30MKK for China and the latest Su-35UB.

Softback, 280 x 215 mm, 128 pages 252 colour photographs, plus 14 pages of colour artworks
1 85780 121 0 **£18.95/US $27.95**

Red Star Volume 3
POLIKARPOV'S I-16 FIGHTER

Yefim Gordon and Keith Dexter

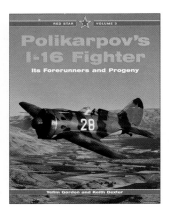

Often dismissed because it did not fare well against its more modern adversaries in the Second World War, Nikolay Polikarpov's I-16 was nevertheless an outstanding fighter – among other things, because it was the world's first monoplane fighter with a retractable undercarriage. Its capabilities were demonstrated effectively during the Spanish Civil War. Covers every variant, from development, unbuilt projects and the later designs that evolved from it.

Sbk, 280 x 215 mm, 128 pages, 185 b/w photographs, 17 pages of colour artworks, plus line drawings
1 85780 131 8 **£18.99/US $27.95**

Red Star Volume 4
EARLY SOVIET JET FIGHTERS

Yefim Gordon

This charts the development and service history of the first-generation Soviet jet fighters designed by such renowned 'fighter makers' as Mikoyan, Yakovlev and Sukhoi, as well as design bureaux no longer in existence – the Lavochkin and Alekseyev OKBs, during the 1940s and early 1950s. Each type is detailed and compared to other contemporary jet fighters. As ever the extensive photo coverage includes much which is previously unseen.

Sbk, 280 x 215 mm, 144 pages 240 b/w and 9 colour photos, 8 pages of colour artworks
1 85780 139 3 **£19.99/US $29.95**

Red Star Volume 5
YAKOVLEV'S PISTON-ENGINED FIGHTERS

Yefim Gordon & Dmitriy Khazanov

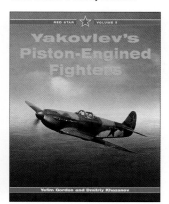

This authoritative monograph describes this entire family from the simple but rugged and agile Yak-1 through the Yak-7 (born as a trainer but eventually developed into a fighter) and the prolific and versatile Yak-9 to the most capable of the line, the Yak-3 with which even the aces of the Luftwaffe were reluctant to tangle. Yak piston fighters also served outside Russia and several examples can be seen in flying condition in the west.

Sbk, 280 x 215 mm, 144 pages, 313 b/w and 2 col photos, 7pp of colour artworks, 8pp of line drawings
1 85780 140 7 **£19.99/US $29.95**

Aerofax
YAKOVLEV Yak-25/26/27/28
Yakovlev's Tactical Twinjets

Yefim Gordon

During the 1950s and 1960s the Soviet design bureau Yakovlev was responsible for a series of swept-wing twin-engined jet combat aircraft, known in the west under various names including *Firebar, Flashlight, Mandrake, Mangrove, Brewer* and *Maestro*. All the various models are covered in this Aerofax – as usual with a mass of new information, detail and illustrations from original Russian sources.

Softback, 280 x 215 mm, 128 pages 202 b/w and 41 colour photographs, plus drawings and 21 colour side-views
1 85780 125 3 **£17.99/US $27.95**

Aerofax
MIKOYAN-GUREVICH MiG-17

Yefim Gordon

The Soviet Union produced and used around 9,000 MiG-17s. First flown in January 1950, it is an extensively upgraded MiG-15 with a redesigned 'scimitar' wing and lengthened fuselage.

It was built under various designations including the Polish Lim-5P and Lim-6bis and the Czech S-105, and served not only with the Soviet armed forces but with other Warsaw Pact nations, seeing combat in the Middle East, in North Vietnam and in Nigeria.

Softback, 280 x 215 mm, 144 pages 172 b/w and 32 colour photo, 10pp of colour sideviews, 12pp of drawings
1 85780 107 5 **£18.99/US $27.95**